COUNTRY MONUMENTS

COUNTRY MONUMENTS
Their Families and Houses

Hugh Collinson

DAVID & CHARLES
NEWTON ABBOT   LONDON
NORTH POMFRET (VT)   VANCOUVER

0 7153 6742 0

Set in 12 on 13pt Bembo
and printed in Great Britain
by Latimer Trend & Company Ltd Plymouth
for David & Charles (Holdings) Limited
South Devon House Newton Abbot Devon

Published in the United States of America
by David & Charles Inc
North Pomfret Vermont 05053 USA

Published in Canada
by Douglas David & Charles Limited
3645 McKechnie Drive West Vancouver BC

CONTENTS

LIST OF ILLUSTRATIONS

PLATES

IN TEXT

The plates listed above are from photographs taken by the author, with the exception of the following which are reproduced, on the pages noted, by kind permission of the copyright holders: National Monuments Record, Crown Copyright, 17 (top), 35, 89; National Portrait Gallery, 18, 53; the Marquess of Bath, 108 (top). The Wadham brasses are reproduced by permission of the Vicar of Ilminster.

ACKNOWLEDGEMENTS

My eyes were first opened to the pleasures of English monumental sculpture through the work of the late Katharine Esdaile, a stimulus subsequently extended by the researches of the late Rupert Gunnis. Today, anyone working in this field is indebted to Sir Nikolaus Pevsner and his team of writers in the *Buildings of England* series, without whom this study would have been almost impossible.

I am grateful to many rectors and vicars who have allowed facilities for photography and who have kindly confirmed details of monuments in places that I have been unable to revisit. My thanks are also due to friends who have provided information, assisted on technical points and generously made translations from the Latin. Special acknowledgement must be made to Mrs Bridget Harrison who has done so much of the typing, and to my wife whose steadfast co-operation in discovering monuments, copying inscriptions and sharing the driving has enabled this study to be undertaken with so much enjoyment.

The following have kindly allowed me to make use of copyright material: Messrs B. T. Batsford; Ernest Benn; J. M. Dent & Sons; Eyre & Spottiswoode; Victor Gollancz; the Hamlyn Publishing Group; Kingsmead Reprints; Macmillan; Penguin Books; Pergamon Press; Pitkin Pictorials; Routledge & Kegan Paul; also Miss Dorothy Stroud, Mr Laurence Whistler and Sir Harry Verney.

INTRODUCTION

Can storied urn or animated bust
Back to its mansion call the fleeting breath?
Thomas Gray, *Elegy Written
in a Country Churchyard*

Although Gray's words suggest the futility of all monuments, the period that produced the 'Elegy' was one in which the 'storied urn and animated bust', together with all the other devices of the monumental sculptor, were particularly successful in recalling the people whose lives make up the story of a locality and the history of a nation. Through their memorials they come alive for us—not only the nobility, statesmen, captains and lawyers, but merchants, craftsmen and country squires, with their wives and children. They are remembered by urns and effigies, their figures standing, kneeling, reclining or recumbent, down to the smallest details of collars and wigs, gloves and shoes, or simply recorded in the elegant lettering of prose or verse. Although the monuments of the Middle Ages are of immense interest, particularly in showing costume and armour, it was after the Reformation that sculptured memorials began to increase in number and variety to represent every walk of life. With Renaissance exuberance or classical restraint they provide a running commentary on three hundred years of history from Elizabeth I to the reign of Victoria.

More than any other visual sources, monuments enable us to picture those who built and furnished the country houses and

9

employed architects and craftsmen, painters, sculptors and landscape-makers, creating what we now know as the English tradition. Portraits may well be more lively and colourful but they do not bear the inscriptions that make sculptured memorials so informative, and portraits are not always and everywhere accessible, yet monuments, except in a few rare instances, are available at all times; you have only to enter a parish church to find unexpected sculptural delights.

There has always been a certain romance about effigies of medieval knights and there has been a great revival of interest in brass rubbing, but in spite of the pioneer work of Katharine Esdaile and Rupert Gunnis we have yet to come to a proper appreciation of what Sacheverell Sitwell called 'the protestant sculpture of the Church of England'. These post-Reformation monuments have historical value and qualities of craftsmanship as important as any brasses and they illustrate an even wider range of English taste and fashion. Fortunately we know more about these people than we do of those in earlier periods. Their portraits are still with us, their houses and gardens, their books and clocks, and we can read their diaries, sit in the pews where they worshipped and explore the parks where they went riding.

The house with its portraits is complementary to the church with its monuments, so painting and sculpture enable us to build up a picture of the personalities behind places, but where the house has been demolished and the church stands all alone, the remaining monuments are of immense value in the understanding of local history. In such places, instead of the figurative meaning in our quotation, we can take Gray's 'mansion' in its literal sense and rejoice in the way in which the 'storied urn' can so potently recall the people who once lived there. Through their monuments we are able to meet them face to face, and on their own ground, for this study in visual history is undertaken not in museums and art galleries but in the proper setting of the English countryside.

Chapter 1

PEOPLE AND PLACES

... a noble monument of the Hon. Mr. Bertie and of his
lady, in white marble well wigg'd ruff'd and cuff'd . . .
Here the Colonel revell'd for some time in family Pomp! and
desired at parting that the Inscription might be copied and
sent to him.

Hon John Byng, on Waldershare, Kent
from *The Torrington Diaries*

When the Hon John Byng undertook his tour into Kent in the
autumn of 1790 his travelling companion was Colonel Bertie,
later 9th Earl of Lindsey, who had a way of looking up his
family connections wherever he went, and as their excursions
extended to several counties those who were persuaded to copy
inscriptions must have been kept busy. But 'family pomp' was
not the only reason for eighteenth-century antiquarians taking
note of monuments: 'wigg'd, ruff'd and cuff'd' indicates an
interest in costume too. At Spilsby, in Lincolnshire, there was
another reason; after the colonel had ordered his usual copies of
the inscriptions on brasses as well as monuments, and after a
dinner in which 'sad cooking spoil'd everything', they went in
search of the old family seat of the Berties and the Willoughbys
at Eresby, just outside the town. They found the avenue still
standing, with gate piers leading to the site of the former house
and gardens.[1] So the monuments led them to discover the deserted
manor which for centuries had been the centre of family life as
well as of artistic activity which produced a fine house and

grounds, the paintings and furnishings long since gone, and the monuments which remained to tell the tale.

Today, those of us who search for history, not always in books but in the things that history has left behind, can go to Spilsby and look upon those glorious monuments and then, like Byng and his companion, we can still find what remains of the avenue with one enormous gate pier still bravely crowned by an urn, a poignant reminder of what has been lost. The story told by these monuments, the avenue and the forsaken urn, does not stop at the melancholy site of Eresby but is continued at Edenham, thirty-five miles away near Bourne, where the monuments of the Berties and Willoughbys of Eresby are continued into the seventeenth and eighteenth centuries when members of the family became earls of Lindsey and dukes of Ancaster. At Spilsby they are in the Willoughby chapel, at Edenham they line the chancel, and it would be hard to find a more instructive lesson in the changing tides of English taste, from the medieval and early Renaissance of the one to the heroic Roman classicism of the other.

At Edenham we need not search for the forlorn fragments of a vanished house, for happily Grimsthorpe Castle is still very much part of the landscape and quite the grandest seat in all Lincolnshire. The road from Bourne to Grantham passes the end of the great avenue and the house can be seen far away along a perspective of noble trees leading the eye to the Vanbrugh front, whose scale and robust baroque character contrast strongly with the pretty gables of the south side built by Charles Brandon, Duke of Suffolk. The link here is that a Willoughby d'Eresby married first the Duke of Suffolk and then Richard Bertie, and the estates of Grimsthorpe and Eresby continued in the family until the burning of the house near Spilsby in 1769. The avenue that gives us the far-off glimpse is evidence of the earlier formal planting at Grimsthorpe, before Capability Brown came in 1771 to bring the park into line with the prevailing taste for informality, forming the vast lake in place of the straight canals.

This was done for the 3rd Duke of Ancaster, whose monument we shall come to later, and whom Brown must have known earlier, for the duke was a signatory to the petition in 1757 pleading for Brown's promotion to Royal Gardener under George II.

The north front of Grimsthorpe Castle contains a hall that is generally considered to be Vanbrugh's most successful interior. This whole project was one of his last works, for he died in 1725, and it follows closely upon his northern buildings at Seaton Delaval and Lumley. When the 1st Duke of Ancaster died in 1723, Vanbrugh had to make certain that this commission would proceed as arranged, under his successor, and he wrote:

> . . . shall wait upon his new Grace of Ancaster in my way, having the honour of an Invitation from him, to consult about his Building; by which I believe he is inclin'd to go upon the General Design I made for his Father last winter . . .[2]

This is where the monuments at Edenham help us to picture the patrons as well as the artists employed at Grimsthorpe, for we can go and see the figure of the 1st Duke (p 17) standing boldly in Roman costume against a superbly carved architectural background which reaches right up to the roof of the church. It is signed 'L. I. Scheemaeckers and H. Cheere. Inven et Fecit. 1728', so by the time this enormous work was completed and the new front of the castle well advanced, Vanbrugh too was dead, and the larger scheme for the whole building, published in *Vitruvius Britannicus*, was never realised. Although we must expect all sorts of variations in the spelling of names at this time, the initials that appear on the signature of this monument are rather puzzling, for it was Henry Scheemakers who was at that time in partnership with Henry Cheere, and it seems incredible that some assistant who cut the lettering would make such an error. There may be some reason for this, as yet undiscovered, or perhaps the carver was just not concentrating when he came to cut the initials, and thereafter nobody noticed.[3] Henry Scheemakers came from Antwerp and was in England for a very short time so his output was small compared with the enormous number of works by his brother Peter, to be found in churches all over the country. The figure on the next monument, of the 2nd Duke of Ancaster who continued the patronage of Vanbrugh, is by one who started as an assistant of Henry Cheere, the French sculptor Roubiliac, and Rupert Gunnis in his *Dictionary of British Sculptors* tells the delightful story of the beginning of his rise to fame. On his way back from Vauxhall one evening Roubiliac picked up a pocket book containing money and papers belonging to Sir Edward Walpole, which he returned to the owner. It was this act of honesty, together with specimens of sculpture that were shown to him, that persuaded Walpole to introduce the young man to Henry Cheere. In view of this episode it is nice to recall that it was for Vauxhall Gardens that Roubiliac later did the figure of Handel as his first independent commission, twenty-three years before the well-known monument to Handel in Westminster Abbey.

But we must return to that ducal chancel at Edenham where we shall find further memorials of importance on the south side. One of these is a sort of monumental family tree which would have pleased the poet Gray, for the central urn is surrounded by no less than seven 'animated busts', but it is the neighbouring work on this side that draws our attention. The 3rd and 4th Dukes of Ancaster died within a year of each other so they share a double monument which is of special interest to us because these noblemen are so differently portrayed, the one who died in 1778 being in the heroic Roman guise of immortality while the other is in contemporary costume with his peer's robes, and holding a lovely medallion of his wife. Was this done because when the design was ordered, from Charles Harris of London, the 4th Duke was still living? This seems to be the most likely explanation and is supported by a similar instance at Coxwold, North Yorkshire, where Thomas Belasyse, Earl of Fauconberg, who died in 1700, wears contemporary costume whereas the accompanying figure of his father, who died more than fifty years earlier, is in Roman garb.

While at Coxwold there are some interesting connections that should be mentioned. The monuments that crowd the narrow chancel are relevant to the beautiful setting of the village, for the landscape is largely that of Newburgh Priory, long owned by the Belasyse family, and an unexpected link with the famous figures of history comes from the fact that Earl Fauconberg's second wife was the daughter of Oliver Cromwell. It is said that the Protector's body was eventually brought to Newburgh. A link with a notable figure of quite a different kind is provided by the memorial to Laurence Sterne, who wrote much of *Tristram Shandy* while he was rector of Coxwold. He was an eccentric man and the inscription tells us that 'STERNE was THE MAN who with gigantic stride mow'd down luxuriant follies far and wide', and that he was 'Ridicul'd, abus'd, By fools insulted and by prudes accus'd', apparently not without cause, but the oddest escapade of all happened after his death in London. It appears that his remains were stolen by body-snatchers but were returned to his grave with the top of the skull missing; some Freemasons then erected a stone with incorrect dates, but this was later corrected by means of a second stone. It was not until 1969 that Sterne was finally laid to rest at Coxwold and the stones re-erected there.[4]

Byng visited Grimsthorpe in the year of the French Revolution but it seems that Colonel Bertie was not with him, which is a pity, for the colonel would certainly have 'revell'd in family pomp' at the castle and at Edenham church, more pleased with himself than Byng seems to have been. On this occasion the diarist was particularly peevish, to use his own expressive word, and he had nothing good to say of the place, but he was hungry and seems to have expected the duke to give him a meal, which to us seems unfair to his Grace. So nothing was right for poor Byng, Vanbrugh's hall was 'in all his clumsy taste', many of the pictures were copies, Capability Brown's lake was considered 'ugly water, upon and near which is neither Tree nor Shrub', which is an interesting comment upon the shaven and shorn appearance of the Brown style after a little more than ten years maturing, and Vanbrugh's chapel was both 'tasteless and devotionless'. Byng's only consolation was that he saw no servants, so was saved from the necessity of giving tips![5] Fortunately things are very different today, and although Grimsthorpe is not normally open, its noble setting can be appreciated by the passing traveller who seeks to complement the sculptural delights of nearby Edenham and far-off Spilsby.

Before we leave the pleasant rolling limestone country of south-west Lincolnshire we must turn to one of those unexpected discoveries that frequently occur in a study of this kind. In the year 1778 when the 3rd Duke of Ancaster died, and Capability Brown's alterations to the park and lake were new features of the estate, there was a boating accident at Grimsthorpe which resulted in the untimely death of a young violinist named Thomas Linley. He came from a very musical family in Bath where his father, also Thomas, was a teacher and composer who organised the concerts in that city but is perhaps best known for being the father of Elizabeth, the beautiful and gifted singer who, after a tempestuous courtship, married Sheridan. She was frequently painted by the artists of the day, including Reynolds and Gainsborough, appearing in these portraits sometimes with her sister or with her brother Thomas whose training in the violin took him to Florence, and it was there that he met the young Mozart. The two boys, both fourteen years of age, became close friends and Mozart later spoke of Thomas Linley as a true genius who would have become 'one of the greatest ornaments of the musical world'. Thomas Linley, the elder, his daughters and an infant daughter of the Sheridans are all commemorated by a memorial, by King of Bath, on the wall of the east walk of the cloisters at Wells Cathedral (p 17). It is an unpretentious tablet, topped with a draped urn and decorated

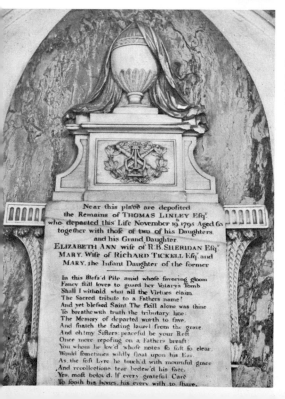

Page 17 (right) Edenham (Lincs).
Detail of the monument to Robert
Bertie, 1st Duke of Ancaster, for whom
Vanbrugh designed the north front of
Grimsthorpe Castle. By Scheemakers
and Cheere, 1728

(left) Wells Cathedral, east walk of
cloisters. Memorial to members of the
Linley family, bearing a reference to
Sheridan. By King of Bath, 1795

Page 18 (above) Penshurst (Kent).
Robert Sidney, 4th Earl of Leicester.
Children who had died are shown as
named cherubs. By William Stanton
and William Woodman, 1704

(right) Lady Anne Clifford. Married
first to the 3rd Earl of Dorset (Knole)
and then to the 4th Earl of Pembroke
(Wilton). Her monument is at Appleby

with musical instruments, the sort of thing that one passes by without a glance because there are thousands like it on the walls of our cathedrals and parish churches, their wording too extravagant in praise or too repetitive in commendation. Yet this modest tablet recalls so much that is of significance in the arts of eighteenth-century England, not only the musical life of Bath but the contemporary work of Sheridan, Reynolds and Gainsborough, the young Mozart in Florence, his young friend whose tragic death at Grimsthorpe led to his burial in the ducal vault at Edenham, and the lovely Elizabeth, of whom Horace Walpole wrote:

> Miss Linley's beauty is in the superlative degree. The King admires her and ogles her as much as he dares to do in so holy a place as an oratorio.[6]

PORTRAITS AND SCULPTURE

If the careful study of monuments, and the associated arts, can reveal a story as unexpected as that which connects Grimsthorpe Castle with Wells Cathedral and touches upon the work of Mozart and Sheridan, Reynolds and Gainsborough as well as Vanbrugh, Roubiliac and Capability Brown, then we can expect a whole world of art patronage to be opened up if we journey from church to church, and from house to house, relating monuments to portraits. This is particularly true of those monuments that are associated with a great country house that is regularly open to the public and offers an abundance of art treasures and historic personalities.

Penshurst Place, in Kent, has long been dear to the hearts of English people, for its great hall is the absolute epitome of the Middle Ages and the long gallery has all the subtle beauty of Elizabethan and Jacobean times. The church lies close to the house, just over the garden wall, and is approached under an archway from a sort of close of cottages; a prettier prelude to a parish church would be hard to imagine. In the Sidney Chapel there is an unusual monument which has a large central urn flanked by two angelic figures who seem to be performing an elegant dance, while in the upper part there is a heavenly flock of cherubs, like winged choristers emerging from breaks in the clouds (p 18). This is no mere artistic device and these little faces with their fluttering wings are not just cherubs from the sculptor's stock-in-trade, for they bear the names of the children of Robert Sidney, 4th Earl of Leicester. Of his fifteen children, nine died young, so this tender memorial to the earl and his countess records their recurrent griefs, with each little flying figure neatly named, except for one, 'The First Childe', which presumably died before baptism. The larger, full-length dancing figures at the sides are also children, Frances and Robert, and it is this son Robert who makes such an interesting link with the portraits in the long gallery at Penshurst Place. Robert Sidney, the father, married Elizabeth Egerton, daughter of the Earl of Bridgewater, and they both have portraits here, attributed to Verelst; the earl wears the long wig of the period and his countess is accompanied by their son Philip who happily survived to become the 5th Earl of Leicester. Another picture attributed to Verelst shows the boy Philip with his sister, and in the sky above them is a little cherub to represent their elder brother Robert who had died at the age of six. So sculptor and painter are using the same motif to commemorate deceased children and it would be nice to know the exact date of the Verelst portrait in relation to the monument, which was begun in 1704. Verelst died in 1702, and so did the 4th Earl whose monument by Stanton followed the theme of cherub children. This probably began as a painter's device for it had been employed earlier by Van Dyck, as we shall see.

Penshurst can show further links between sculptors and painters, churches and country houses. William Stanton, the designer of the 4th Earl's monument, did not include figures of that nobleman and his wife, which we may think a pity because amongst his works there are some figure sculptures of a very high order. One thinks of the exquisite Shirburne group at Mitton, near Stonyhurst in Lancashire, Lord Rivers at Macclesfield and the Earl of Coventry at Elmley Castle, which we shall be considering later. The Stanton family business was in Holborn where three generations produced some of the finest monuments of the period from the Restoration to George I. We shall meet them again at Belton, Lincolnshire, where William Stanton was master mason for Sir John Brownlow's beautiful house. He died soon after starting the Penshurst monument and strangely it was completed not by his son in the same business but by William Woodman whose masterpiece is the Newhaven memorial at Drayton Beauchamp, Bucks. Sir Philip Sidney, the famous poet, soldier and courtier, was not buried at Penshurst, for he had a state funeral at Old St Paul's and his memorial perished with so many others in the Great Fire of 1666, but there are several portraits of him in the house together with countless other Sidneys whose portraits make some interesting connections with monuments that we shall find in places far away from this lovely corner of Kent. In the dining-room there are paintings of Robert Dudley, Earl of Leicester, Queen Elizabeth's 'Robin', whose grand tomb we shall visit later at Warwick, and the poet's daughter whom we shall see again as a countess on the 5th Earl of Rutland's monument at Bottesford, in Leicestershire. Yet another instance of the widespread connections of this family is recalled in the long gallery by the portrait of Sir Henry Sidney, the poet's father, whose marriage established the Dudley relationship. He was Lord President of the Council of the Welsh Marches, with headquarters at Ludlow Castle where he added the Elizabethan building at the entrance. While the family was living there his daughter Ambrosia died and was given a handsome heraldic memorial in the chancel of Ludlow church. This has recently been recoloured and gilded, so the heraldic achievements of Sidney and Dudley, more commonly associated with Penshurst and with that splendid timbered hospital by the west gate of Warwick, glow unexpectedly here amongst other recoloured monuments connected with the Council of the Marches in that stately church.

The porcupine that is the crest of the Sidneys seems far from home in the one-time capital of the Welsh Border, but we must expect this sort of thing as we follow the work of sculptors and painters from place to place among the scattered properties of the patrons who employed them. That same porcupine was borne upon the helmet of Sir Philip Sidney at his funeral and can now be seen in the hall at Penshurst, but this poor creature is covered with holes where the quills were once inserted, and only a few blunted ones are left. Again on the tomb of his daughter at Bottesford, amongst the splendour of the earls of Rutland, we see the same animal, looking like a dog with holes, but if we wish to recapture the true glory of this family crest we must go to the Chapel of St Paul on the north side of the choir at Westminster Abbey. Here the monument to Frances Sidney, Countess of Sussex, has replaced the altar and goes towering up towards the vault, all glittering with gold and colour, ten times more spectacular than her niece's small tomb at Ludlow, and the animal at her feet is brilliant blue with long, gilded spines. As one would expect, her dainty feet are not quite resting upon this prickly creature. Frances was aunt to Sir Philip and she founded Sidney Sussex College at Cambridge where there is a full-length portrait of her behind the high table in the hall.

Our journeys now take us to another of the country houses of southern England, to Wilton, the seat of that branch of the Herbert family from which came the earls of Pembroke. Perhaps the best-known feature here is the Double Cube Room, and deservedly so, for it is one of the most exquisite interiors in any English house, the culmination of the suite of state rooms designed by Inigo Jones and completed by Webb. Most of the west wall is occupied by Van Dyck's painting of the family of the 4th Earl, and further Van Dycks adorn the other walls amidst gilded settings of the utmost splendour, a tribute to the patronage of the arts at Wilton during the time of the two brothers, William and Philip Herbert, 3rd and 4th Earls of Pembroke. Such patronage appealed to Charles I and Henrietta Maria who 'loved Wilton above all places and went there every summer', and some years earlier the first folio of Shakespeare's plays was dedicated to 'this most noble and incomparable paire of Brethren'.[7] But Wilton had been a centre of the arts even before that incomparable pair. Their mother was Mary, the sister of Sir Philip Sidney, and sister also to Ambrosia of the Ludlow monument, so here we find a link between Penshurst and that far-off castle amongst the Shropshire hills where Mary spent much of her childhood until Queen Elizabeth took her into the royal household and Robert Dudley arranged the marriage that brought her to Wilton. Sir Philip Sidney spent a lot of time with his sister at Wilton which became, says Aubrey 'like a college, there were so many learned and ingeniose persons'.[8] Among them were Ben Jonson, Edmund Spenser and Samuel Daniel, whom we shall meet again later.

Towards the end of her life Mary, Countess of Pembroke, was given the royal manor of Ampthill in Bedfordshire, by James I, and on part of the estate, at Houghton Conquest, she built a mansion. Today its ruins stand high on the greensand ridge overlooking the plain, but they are being cared for by the Department of the Environment so decay is arrested and there is public access. If you are travelling by rail between St Pancras and Bedford you have a good view of the ruins if you keep a sharp look-out on the right-hand side after the train has emerged from Ampthill Tunnel. First there is the handsome Ampthill House, its light stone façade standing effectively against the wooded hills, and then, much farther away, you see the strange silhouette of Houghton on the skyline, like broken teeth, and it is hard to believe that tradition asserts that this was once the 'House Beautiful' of *Pilgrim's Progress*, for today it is a melancholy ruin that looks down on Bunyan's Elstow in the level landscape below. We too can look down on Elstow, and all the dim blue

23

distances of Bedfordshire, if we take the field road to the ruins and stand in the windy spaces of the colonnade, recalling the woman who knew Penshurst, Ludlow, the court of Elizabeth and the earlier Wilton before its present splendours. She died in 1621 and was buried beside her husband in the family vault at Salisbury Cathedral, but, like the other Pembrokes that rest there, she has no monument, so instead we must be content with the lovely epitaph that was published with some of her son's poems and which has been variously attributed to Ben Jonson and William Browne:

> Underneath this marble hearse
> Lies the subject of all verse;
> Sidney's sister, Pembroke's mother.
> Death! ere thou hast slain another
> Wise and fair and good as she
> Time shall throw a dart at thee.[9]

The vast canvas by Van Dyck that dominates the Double Cube Room incorporates the motif of flying cherubs to denote children of the 4th Earl of Pembroke who had died in infancy, a use of this delightful device half a century earlier than its occurrence at Penshurst in the long gallery and in Stanton's memorial in the church. Is it too fanciful to suppose that this charming way of remembering these children suggested itself to later Sidneys because of their familiarity with this distinguished precedent in the house of their kinsmen? The Van Dyck group has other links with monuments, making this astonishing room at Wilton a starting-point for further connections within the field of seventeenth-century art in England. The beautifully posed figure that seems to come forward almost on to the frame, in front of Pembroke's family, is his daughter-in-law, Lady Mary Villiers, whose father was the infamous Duke of Buckingham, murdered in the presence of Pembroke at Portsmouth in 1628. She also appears as a child on her parents' monument in Henry VII's

Chapel at Westminster, and then her mother, of the West-minster monument, appears again as a child on *her* parents' tomb at Bottesford, as we shall discover later. The costume changes involved in this sort of family sequence are quite fascinating.

The main figures of the Duke of Buckingham's memorial at Westminster are by Le Sueur who did so many bronzes of Charles I, including the equestrian figure at the top of White-hall. Then we meet Le Sueur again in yet another link with the Double Cube Room, for the portrait on the left of the fireplace, of the 3rd Earl of Pembroke, has its counterpart in the Old Bodleian Quadrangle at Oxford where Le Sueur's dark figure of this same earl stands nobly on a pedestal, against a repeat pattern of panelling in honey-coloured stone. His brother Philip, the head of the family in Van Dyck's group, seems to take rather a back seat in the picture as if anxious to exhibit to full advantage the children of his first wife who disport themselves around him, while by his side and also rather in the shadows sits his second countess, with folded arms, as if disapproving of all the activities of her step-children, their partners, and the sweet cherubs that flutter and tumble in a cloudy sky.

FROM KENT TO CUMBRIA

The sober countess who sits, so substantial and inscrutable, beside her lord, presiding over all the gilded gaiety of that room at Wilton, is the famous Lady Anne Clifford (p 18), a character who reminds us of Bess of Hardwick, for she married into noble families, disputed her inheritance, became immensely wealthy and undertook the most ambitious building activities in her old age, becoming quite a legend in her time. Before coming to Wilton she was married to Richard Sackville, 3rd Earl of Dorset, and with her husband she ruled over the great house of Knole. If we read V. Sackville-West's book *Knole and the Sackvilles* we shall enjoy extracts from Lady Anne's diaries that give a vivid picture of this remarkable character, also a catalogue of the household at Knole showing how the tables were allocated in the hall in order to accommodate the staff of that enormous house. Portraits of Anne Clifford and Richard Sackville, attributed to William Larkin, hang on either side of the fireplace in the gracious ballroom at Knole, while in the great hall there is one of Edward, the 4th Earl of Dorset, whose 'reign' followed that of Lady Anne and her husband. This picture always evokes special comment because the earl's key of office as Lord Chamberlain to Charles I is shown in the painting while the actual key hangs from the edge of the frame.

We move from painting to sculpture again when we consider Richard Sackville the son of Edward, the Cavalier earl and Lord Chamberlain. Richard married Frances daughter of Lionel Cranfield, 1st Earl of Middlesex, who has that lordly tomb which forms the centrepiece of St Benedict's Chapel at Westminster. Through this marriage many of the loveliest things at Knole came into the Sackville family, including the great portrait of Lionel Cranfield by Mytens, and the copies of the Raphael Cartoons. But our main concern is an outstanding piece of sculpture that forms the centrepiece of another chapel, not at Westminster but at Withyham, in Sussex, which has long been the traditional resting-place of the Sackvilles because their earlier seat, Buckhurst, lies in this parish. Richard, 5th Earl of Dorset, and his Cranfield countess kneel on either side of the tomb of their youngest son Thomas, 'the thirteenth child and seventh son who in his thirteenth year his race had run'. It is one of the most moving memorials that we shall find on any of our journeys and is important because it marks a new step towards dramatic realism in English monumental art (p 35). This work is also of special significance because records tell us that it was made by C. G. Cibber and it had to be done to 'ye well liking of Mr. Peter Lilly', His Majesty's painter.[10] When we look at this lovely group, and the exquisitely carved head of the earl, comparing it with his portrait in the ballroom at Knole, it is hard to believe that as a patron he was so unsure of his sculptor that the design had to be approved by an established painter.

But we must return to Lady Anne Clifford who died the year before Thomas Sackville, and whose later life took her from Knole to Wilton and then finally back to her inherited estates in the north. Neither of her marriages seems to have been very happy. Perhaps this accounts for her grave expression in the Van Dyck painting, and in later life she wrote, 'the marble pillars of Knowle in Kent and Wilton in Wiltshire were to me often times but the gay arbour of anguish'.[11] Perhaps she was happier when, after being widowed for the second time, she returned to her own countryside and her own people at Appleby, and engaged in a vigorous programme of building activity. In defiance of Cromwell she restored her six castles and made a point of living in each of them at fixed times, dispensing charity and hospitality, so Appleby, Brougham, Brough, Pendragon, Skipton and Barden Tower saw this so-called 'Queen of the North' at regular intervals, making her royal progress as V. Sackville-West tells us in her extracts from Lady Anne's diaries: '. . . travelling in her horse-litter, her ladies in her coach-and-six, her menservants on horseback, her women in other coaches, and a rabble of small fry following, so that the miniature army which accompanied her amounted sometimes to as many as three hundred.'[12]

In one sense we can still follow Lady Anne today, especially if we travel down the upper Eden from Aisgill, on the Yorkshire–Cumbria boundary, and past the scattered farms to Pendragon Castle. There are only a few broken fragments now, but the setting is lovely with the tilted scarp of Wild Boar Fell rising steeply on one side, and, facing it across the valley, the long line of Mallerstang Edge. Above Pendragon the sheep farms are patterned with stone walls and then the fields give way to the open moor, and here, unbelievably high on the mountainside, runs the railway line from Carlisle over to Settle and Skipton. The trains are suitably dwarfed by the scale of the scenery in the upper vale of Eden, but lower down at Brough it is a different story. The road traffic coming over the Pennines on the A66 has left no peace in this village, yet the setting is still grand and Lady Anne's castle is a four-square mass of warm red stone, with a more distant southward background of the sharp edges of Mallerstang and Wild Boar Fell. Northwards we find Cross Fell making a mountain background to Appleby and here we are very much in the presence of Lady Anne, for her castle stands at the top of Boroughgate, her church, where she lies with her mother, at the bottom, and her almshouses at one side of this comely street. Moreover there are tall pillars, top and bottom, the Moot Hall on an island site, and a rather unexpected 'Gothick' screen or cloister leading into the churchyard at the foot of the hill with the church itself closing the vista; in all, a remarkably fine piece of townscape.

As well as founding the almshouses Lady Anne rebuilt the chancel of Appleby church and built or remodelled churches at Brough, Brougham, Ninekirk and Mallerstang, near her castles, during the 1650s and 1660s in an interesting Gothic Survival style. At Brougham Castle, near Penrith, the river Eamont prattles over boulders on its way from Ullswater to the Eden, the dipper sings amongst the wet stones, letting the water run over his back, and the proud walls of this splendid ruin are rose-red above meadows of brightest green. This is gentler country, where the hills stand back, the Pennines to the east and the Lake mountains westward, and now that the old Eamont Bridge and the sharp corner by the castle have been bypassed, the new stretch of road gives a better view of Brougham than ever before, and the whole place looks like a nineteenth-century watercolour. Some distance along the main road to Appleby, and still mercifully preserved in spite of road widening, there stands a curious pillar with sundial, heraldry and inscription, which is yet another reminder of Lady Anne for it was erected by her in 1656 at the spot where she had said her last farewell to her mother, forty years before. The other monument to her

28

mother, in Appleby church, is a most distinguished piece of sculpture with fine detailing and a metal coronet, the inscription reminding us that she was a Russell from Chenies, in Buckinghamshire, daughter of the 2nd Earl of Bedford whose own monument is amongst that wonderful series in Chenies church. She married George Clifford who became 3rd Earl of Cumberland, best known to art historians as the subject of Nicholas Hilliard's exquisite little picture in the National Maritime Museum, Greenwich, showing the earl as Queen Elizabeth's champion, his gauntlet flung down and the queen's glove pinned to his hat. His monument is at Skipton, a plain black slab upon an altar tomb, so once again sculpture and painting help to recreate the figures of history, in places so different and so far apart.

Also in quite different places and far apart are two further memorials erected by Lady Anne Clifford, both to poets. One is to Edmund Spenser in Westminster Abbey, originally by Nicholas Stone but since renewed, and the other is to Samuel Daniel who is said to have succeeded Spenser as poet laureate in 1599. We have already met Daniel at Wilton where he was one of the literary circle patronised by Mary Sidney, Countess of Pembroke, and he was tutor to her son William, the one with the Le Sueur statue in the Old Bodleian Quadrangle at Oxford. Later, Samuel Daniel became tutor to Anne Clifford when she was a child in her father's castle at Skipton, so it is nice to know that she remembered him, even though it was more than forty years after his death in 1619 that she put up his memorial at Beckington, Somerset. You discover this only if you can manage to read the rather obscure inscription on the wall in the north aisle of Beckington church, beneath a bust of Daniel:

. . . that excellent poet and historian who was tutor to the Lady Anne Clifford in her youth . . . who in gratitude to him erected this monument to his memory a long time after, when she was Countess Dowager of Pembroke, Dorset and Montgomery . . .

29

She did not become Countess Dowager of Pembroke until 1650 when the builder of the Double Cube Room died, so the 'long time after', together with Daniel's reputation as poet laureate, may account for the rare combination of the little 'Van Dyck beard' with the laurel-wreathed head and Roman toga, which are so much more characteristic of post-Restoration classicism. Lady Anne's remarkable life ended in 1676 and she was buried at Appleby near to her mother. Unfortunately there is no effigy, but a stately tomb against the wall is decorated with a collection of shields that must be a delight, and a challenge, to the student of heraldry. Like her mother, who had died exactly a month after Shakespeare, Lady Anne spent her last hours at Brougham, perhaps the most impressive of all those castles to which she journeyed unceasingly after her return from those gentler country houses of the south which had been to her 'often times but the gay arbour of anguish'. The poet Gray visited her tomb in 1767 and wrote these lines as part of his own epitaph for her:

> Now clean, now hideous, mellow now, now gruff,
> She swept, she Hiss'd, she ripen'd and grew rough
> At Brougham, Pendragon, Appleby and Brough.[13]

It would have been good to have seen an effigy of her upon her tomb, perhaps carved with as much skill as was her kinsman's beautiful monument at Withyham in the following year, or as accomplished as her mother's, so near hers but sixty years earlier. Then we could have compared Lady Anne's features with her portrait at Knole in all her finery as Countess of Dorset, or with the meditative matron at Wilton in that gorgeous room that seems to us so very different from the castles of the north where now, as then, the wind blows cold from Wild Boar Fell and Mallerstang.

Chapter 2

MONUMENTS
AND LANDSCAPE-MAKERS

If you want a monument to his devotion to God, look around at this sacred abode, raised and embellished at the expense that befits the man himself.

From the epitaph of the 6th Earl of Coventry,
Croome d'Abitot

The original Latin of the Earl of Coventry's epitaph at Croome is much longer than the brief extract given above, and it goes some way towards explaining how devotion to God comes to be part of the landscaping of the Croome estate. In short, he provided work for the poor, or as the inscription says, freely translated: '. . . he displayed a benevolent attitude towards those who had less means than he had, so that he abundantly helped them in their misfortune and vigorously roused them to work, thus making them good citizens'. Not all memorials to landowners make claims of this kind, but there are many that make reference to the planting that went on all over England in that remarkable eighteenth century so that, in countless parishes, when the squire or peer was laid to rest in the little church in the park, the face of the land was very different from what it had been when he took up his inheritance.

To find Croome d'Abitot we must go to the triangle of country made by the meeting of the Avon and the Severn, between Pershore and Tewkesbury. On one side, that massive outlier of the Cotswolds, Bredon Hill, thrusts its bulk into the

31

Severn Vale, and on the other the prospect is closed by the dramatic outline of the Malvern Hills. It was here that the 6th Earl of Coventry transformed a marshy tract, that was the old home of the family, into an estate worthy of the best traditions of English eighteenth-century taste. Robert Adam, Capability Brown and Sanderson Miller all seem to have played their part in the Coventry project, but it is rather difficult to determine just where Miller came into it. Croome Court is very similar to his Hagley Hall and there are letters that show that he was involved at some stage, yet Brown appears to have been the designer of the house as well as of its princely setting which— in spite of the wilderness of Defford airfield, the coming of the M5 motorway, and the house suffering a change of use—still remains a noble landscape to be enjoyed by those of us who are willing to do some 'mapwork' and explore by-roads that surround the estate. The earl had begun the transformation of the grounds before he succeeded to the estate, the house was started in 1751, and then Adam was working here, doing park ornaments as well as the interiors, off and on for thirty years from 1760. It is fortunate that we can catch a contemporary glimpse of all this in Richard Wilson's painting in Birmingham Art Gallery, showing the house by the lake, a bridge, a rotunda in the park and the new church on the hill. Adam and Brown seem to have collaborated on the church, which was re-sited in 1763 to form a pretty 'Gothick' eye-catcher, re-housing the great series of Coventry monuments moved from the earlier building.

Birmingham Art Gallery also has a full-length portrait of the 6th Earl of Coventry, by Allan Ramsay, which is helpful because by the time the earl's monument was made, in 1809, we have reached the period of the draped urn and mourning female figure (p 35), far removed from the contemporary costume of the monuments of a hundred years earlier which help us to visualise the landowners of that period. This memorial by the younger Bacon tells us something of the earl's 'fine intellect,

skill at landscaping, courteous disposition and elegant and agree-
able person' as well as his benevolent attitude to the poor. He
married Maria, the elder of the Gunning sisters, and brought his
bride to Croome which was already becoming an appropriate
setting for one of the most beautiful women of the time. Her
beauty caused her to be mobbed when she appeared in Hyde
Park, so the king gave her a guard of two sergeants with halberds,
and twelve soldiers.[1] Maria, who was considered the more
comely but less intelligent, had a shoemaker in Worcester who
made two and a half guineas by charging the public a penny for
a peep at her shoes. When she died at the age of twenty-seven,
10,000 people went to see her coffin,[2] but the earl's second wife
is remembered in a very different way; of the thousands who
enjoy the panorama of coloured counties from Broadway
Tower, on the crest of the Cotswolds, few will realise that it is an
eye-catcher originally designed to be seen by the Countess of
Coventry from her windows at Croome, nearly fifteen miles
away.

Accounts survive regarding the furnishing of Croome Court,
and Geoffrey Beard in his *Georgian Craftsmen* recalls for us the
names of those who worked there, providing clocks and carpets,
doors and ceilings, furniture and fireplaces. On one occasion
when the earl made some deductions from the bill of charges
for work done, Adam felt compelled to make a complaint to
his lordship, whereupon the full amount was paid the same day.
The two men remained good friends, so much so that the earl
was a pall-bearer at Adam's funeral in 1792. It was from the
earl's London house in Piccadilly that Capability Brown was
returning home when he collapsed and died, and eventually a
memorial to Brown was erected near the lake that he had made
at Croome:

To the memory of Lancelot Brown who by the powers of his
inimitable and creative genius formed this garden scene out of a
morass.[3]

Brown was laid to rest at Fenstanton, near Huntingdon, and Adam in Westminster Abbey, but their patron the 6th Earl of Coventry was appropriately buried at Croome where his epitaph bids us look around if we seek a really fitting monument. An apt memorial it certainly is if we go and stand to the west of the church, under the pretty little tower that appears in the background of Richard Wilson's painting, and look down to the court and lake below. The new position chosen for the church enables it to be approached from the village by a secret path through an orchard at the back, a discreet access for ordinary folk, unseen from the house, and an approach with just that element of surprise that adds enormously to the enjoyment of discovering this memorable spot. The interior has an air of fantasy, for the Adamesque interpretation of Gothic is quite unreal, while the solemn series of superb monuments makes us tread softly in the presence of so much beauty. Yet this is a place that you might never find without a large-scale map, and it emphasises the necessity of patiently searching for some obscure public path to a hidden church in order to gain a good view of a house and estate that it not open to the public. As we discovered at Grimsthorpe, there is usually one point at which a road crosses a vista and gives us a distant prospect of the house, and again 'mapwork' will indicate these vantage-points. There are many such estates, but some that come to mind are Badminton, Belton, Wimpole, Holkham, Woburn, Windsor, Castle Ashby and Burghley, most of which are open at some time, but the surprise view is a delight on other days and in all seasons. Croome is no exception; a distant view can be obtained from the lane near High Green and several of the park buildings can be seen from the motorway and the lanes that cross it, but the most exciting discovery awaits the enthusiast who explores the roads to the south of the estate where, on a lane leading off the A4104 between Pershore and Upton-on-Severn, in an open field by the roadside, stands Dunstall Castle. Unlike most mock castles it is not on a hilltop with windy prospects far and wide,

Page 35 (*above*) Withyham (Sussex). Thomas Sackville, son of the 5th Earl and Countess of Dorset. By C. G. Cibber, 1677

(*left*) Croome d'Abitot (Hereford and Worcs). The 6th Earl of Coventry, for whom Adam and Capability Brown worked together to create the landscape referred to on this monument. By John Bacon the younger, 1809

Page 36 (left) Croome d'Abitot (Hereford and Worcs). Detail of the monument to the 4th Baron Coventry. The crown offered by Faith has been lost but the baron's discarded coronet remains below. By Grinling Gibbons, 1690

(below) Elmley Castle (Hereford and Worcs). In the front, children from the Savage monument, 1631. Behind, the 1st Earl of Coventry whose monument, by William Stanton, was unacceptable at Croome and was erected here in 1700

there are no exaggerated claims of seven counties seen on a clear day, but it remains one of the best of all castle follies, romantic, with immensely tall arches and shattered towers, full of jack-daws and melancholy.

But we have come to Croome to look at monuments as well as landscapes, so we must return to the church in the park and devote some time to the chancel to which the 6th Earl brought the tombs of his ancestors, to make one of the most notable groups of monumental sculpture in the whole country. It is a sort of English version of the Medici Chapel at San Lorenzo, in Florence, and although from the point of view of worship it might be thought unsuitable for a small chancel to be treated like a family mortuary chapel, the effect is undeniably impressive and much of the sculpture is of a very high order. On the south side Thomas, 1st Baron Coventry, reclines between seated figures of Justice and Truth while in front of him are his insignia of office as Lord Keeper of the Great Seal. This fine monument, and the one on the other side of the chancel with an exquisite figure of a young mother and her baby, are from that decade of the 1630s, during the reign of Charles I, which produced the greatest achievements in English monumental sculpture. Much of it, if not by Nicholas Stone or his studio, was certainly influenced by him. There is a link here between Croome and Longleat, for the daughter of Thomas, 1st Baron Coventry, married a Thynne, and this accounts for the Longleat portraits of the Keeper of the Great Seal and his son and daughter which hang in that great Wiltshire house.[4] The son, Sir William Coventry, has no memorial at Croome for he died in Kent and is buried at Penshurst church where there is a mural monument in the south aisle, not far from the Sidney Chapel that we considered earlier. It is always good to meet the characters in Pepys's diary, and this makes Sir William Coventry's memorial and portrait doubly interesting, for Pepys mentions his friend being knighted and becoming a Privy Councillor, his attempted duel with the

Duke of Buckingham and subsequent imprisonment in the Tower, where Pepys frequently visited him.

Contemporary with Pepys's friend Sir William, the reigning Coventry at Croome was John, the 4th Baron, who has the largest of all the monuments there. Lord Coventry reclines between two life-size standing figures of Faith and Hope, not comfortably like his predecessor with the Great Seal of England, but contorted in such a way that he can stretch out a hand towards Faith (p 36). Until recently the whole thing was made more ungainly, and indeed made to look ridiculous, by the fact that the baron had his coronet balanced precariously on his head, though several sizes too small for him. Fortunately there is documentary evidence that the coronet should be at his feet, discarded in favour of a celestial crown that he should really be receiving from Faith, in that outstretched hand. In David Green's life of Grinling Gibbons there is the following extract from the contract for this remarkable monument, made between Gibbons and the young baron's mother in 1690.

> . . . the said late Lord Coventry in all his barons robes lying upon a tomb properly adorned with his coronet tumbled at his feet and his right hand stretched out to catch at a starry crown presented towards him by the serene statue representing Faith . . . and the name of the said Grinling Gibbons to be engraved in some convenient place as the artificer of the said monument.[5]

The starry crown has disappeared, which rather spoils the effect of the gesture to Faith, but happily the coronet has now been taken down from the position for which it was never intended, though there is still a tell-tale mark upon the baron's head where it had been for too long, perhaps ever since Adam and Brown had these tombs carried up the hill from the old church. It is a pity that after this rare instance of a signature being demanded by the patroness, Gibbons seems to have forgotten to sign his work.

Before we leave this corner of Worcestershire there is another story concerning men and monuments that must claim our attention, and it is a strange one. Just as we found that Pepys's friend, Sir William Coventry, had no memorial at Croome but was discovered unexpectedly at Penshurst, so we must look elsewhere for a monument to the 5th Baron, who became the 1st Earl. To find it we must cross the Avon either at Eckington or Pershore and then make our way by devious lanes under the northern flank of Bredon Hill to the lovely village of Elmley Castle, where the Savage family once had a fine house. Their house has gone, but the Savage monument in the church at Elmley Castle is one of the best things in all Worcestershire, its detail as exquisite as that of the mother and child we saw at Croome, for here again is a baby in its mother's arms and all the delightful intricacy of seventeenth-century lace and ribbons. These two mothers, and the comparable masterpiece at Bramfield in Suffolk, which we know to be by Nicholas Stone (see p 128), make three of the most poignant expressions in sculpture from the reign of Charles I, and the Elmley Castle group may be thought to be the highest achievement of that brilliant period. There are so many figures; three recumbent adults and four kneeling sons, on all of whom the student of costume will find collars and fastenings of incredible richness, and all so accessible and easy to examine in a good light from a near-by window. But there is enjoyment of a different kind to be had from the huge monument of the 1st Earl of Coventry who died in the last year of the seventeenth century. The style of the whole composition, with details of the curling periwig and fine lace cravat, the attendant allegorical figures and the towering superstructure, makes a most instructive comparison with the earlier Savage group only a few feet away (p 36). It is in situations like this that we realise the differences in artistic tradition within one century. With the Civil War and so much else intervening between Charles I and William III it makes nonsense of over-simplified expressions such as 'seventeenth-century art'.

The Coventry monument is by William Stanton, whose work

we saw at Penshurst, and it is only at Elmley Castle because, on
being taken to Croome, there seems to have been a family row
which resulted in the new earl not allowing it to stand with those
of his ancestors in the family church, the old one that was lower
down near the former Croome Court. The dowager countess
who had paid for this great work and had it brought all the way
from the Stanton workshop in Holborn must have been placed
in a very embarrassing position. However, she was married
again later, this time to Thomas Savage who agreed to give it a
place amongst his own forebears at Elmley Castle. So the finely
carved pieces, presumably in several waggons, took the road
again to their final home beneath Bredon Hill.[6] There is a
happier side to this story in that Stanton's figure of the 1st Earl
is in a comfortable reclining position at Elmley Castle rather
than the awkward twist of the Gibbons figure of the 4th Baron
at Croome, and he is pointing proudly at his newly acquired
coronet. It is as if he were emphasising the fact that, although he
is separated from his kinsmen across the Avon, he has at least
gained an earldom for the family.

From Elmley Castle you can climb to the top of Bredon Hill
and look westwards to where the dark woods of Croome lie
between the Avon and the Severn. Unlike Penshurst, Knole and
Wilton, few people know of Croome, for it is no longer a stately
home. Its very existence is unsuspected by the majority of
travellers on the motorway as it threads its way between Adam's
temples and Brown's lake, for the highway is discreetly hidden
from house, church and mock castle. The people pass by, like
strangers in the park, of necessity preoccupied and unseeing,
except perhaps for a glimpse of the Panorama tower standing
boldly against the background of the Malvern Hills.

PATRONS AND CRAFTSMEN

Whatever part Sanderson Miller may have played in the planning of the Earl of Coventry's schemes at Croome, there are

other landscapes in which he certainly had a major role. He was one of those 'gentleman amateurs' of the eighteenth century who, in an age of classical taste, turned to the excitement and romance that Gothic could offer, and well before Horace Walpole's Strawberry Hill he was early in the field with his 'Gothick' improvements to his own home at Radway in 1745, the tower on Edgehill above Radway, the mock castles at Hagley and Wimpole, and later a handsome 'Gothick' remodelling of the great hall at Lacock Abbey. He could also produce designs in the accepted classical manner, as shown by Hagley Hall and the Shire Hall at Warwick. Because of Sanderson Miller's influence on landscape and his place in the Romantic movement we must look for his memorial, which we shall find in the church at Radway, just below the wooded escarpment of Edgehill on which his well-known tower still forms a prominent feature of the skyline above the Warwickshire plain. His tablet is high up on the wall inside the church tower and is not easy to find, or to read, but the ladder up to the belfry helps us to decipher it.

For his work at the Shire Hall at Warwick, Miller had the collaboration of William and David Hiorne the masons and architects who, like the Smiths of Warwick before them, were responsible for a great many fine buildings during the eighteenth century. If we add the work of William's son, Francis, then the contribution of the Hiorne family to the Midland landscape is considerable and, once again, we have good reason to search among the tablets in the south transept at St Mary's, Warwick, for memorials to William Hiorne, alderman, 1776, and Francis Hiorne his son, alderman, 1789.[7] Both father and son were mayors of Warwick, Francis three times, even though he died at the early age of forty-five. Foremost among their buildings, and in each case adding a distinctive quality to the landscape, are the churches of Daventry; Tardebigge, with a needle-sharp spire rising beautifully above the lockgates on the Worcester and Birmingham Canal; and one that many will consider to be the most inspired church to be built in Gothic since the Middle Ages, at Tetbury in Gloucestershire.

To turn for a moment to gardeners rather than builders, we shall find in the churchyard at Lambeth, in London, a table tomb with bold relief carvings, not only of trees but of animals and grotesque monsters which seem strange devices with which to commemorate a family of gardeners until we remember that John Tradescant established his famous 'Ark' at Lambeth, in about 1629. This was a collection of animals as well as plants, perhaps the first to be worthy of the name 'museum', and it eventually became the nucleus of the Ashmolean Museum at Oxford, where there is a room of treasures devoted to the memory of the Tradescants. John, the elder, was employed by Robert Cecil, Earl of Salisbury, and it is thought that the figure of a gardener with rake and flower basket, carved on one of the newel posts of the staircase at Hatfield House, probably represents Tradescant. He travelled widely in search of plants, even joining trade missions and military expeditions just because of the botanical opportunities they offered. For a time he was in the service of the Duke of Buckingham and then became gardener to Charles I and Henrietta Maria, a position in which he was succeeded by John the younger, while yet a third John had died young. Their epitaph at St Mary's, Lambeth, is worth quoting:

> Know, stranger, e'er thou pass, beneath this stone
> Lie John Tradescant, grandsire, father, son . . .
> These famous antiquarians that had been
> Both gardeners to the rose and lily Queen,
> Transplanted now themselves, sleep here; and when
> Angels shall with their trumpets waken men,
> And fire shall purge the world, these hence shall rise
> And change their gardens for a Paradise.

From that era of brilliant architects and craftsmen, the age of Wren and Grinling Gibbons, two memorials come to mind as representing men who carried out work for which the credit is usually given to their better-known masters. At Burford, close to the Cotswold stone quarries at Taynton, there is a mural monument to Christopher Kempster, one of the great masons of his time. Some of the local sources of stone are still known as Kitts' Quarries, and Kempster's house is inscribed with his name and date 1698. Wren said he could rely on him because he was 'a very able man, modest, honest and treatable'.[8] Kempster's epitaph describes him as

> . . . Freeman of the City of London and of ye Company of Masons. He was a person Eminent in his profession and Built several Churches in the said City and was many Years employ'd in Building the Cathedral and Dome of St. Pauls . . .

The interior decoration of a great house such as Chatsworth, Petworth or Burghley involved a considerable team of craftsmen, as did the vast projects at St Paul's and Blenheim, and research has now revealed the names of several of these men. Much of the work popularly supposed to be by Grinling Gibbons has been found to be by others, with or without the master's overall responsibility for the decorative scheme. The superb wood-carving at Chatsworth is now known to have been carried out by Samuel Watson, the resident craftsman who worked there for most of his life, so it is nice to find a tribute to him on his memorial at Heanor, in Derbyshire, where he died in 1715.

> Watson is Gone
> Whose skilfull art display'd
>   To the very life
> Wt'ever nature made.
> View but his wondrous Works
>   In Chatsworth Hall
>   Which are so gaiz'd at
> And admired by all.
>   Your'l say tis pity
> He should hidden lye
>   And nothing said
> T'revive his memory.

There are other monuments on which the inscriptions mention the building or planting activities of the person commemorated, but in most instances, as we have seen in the case of the 6th Earl of Coventry, these are patrons who employed architects and landscape men, rather than the artists themselves. At Acton, in Suffolk, the monument to Robert Jennens, adjutant of the Duke of Marlborough, 1722, tells us that 'he purchased the estate and began the house'. It is a pity the house has gone, except for some subsidiary building, for this is an exceptionally fine work, possibly by Thomas Green of Camberwell, and it has details of costume just as superbly cut as those on the famous brass of Sir Robert de Bures, a few yards away. But how many of the hundreds of brass rubbers, who now have to 'pre-book' their hour or two of time on Sir Robert, spare a moment to admire the masterpiece of sculpture on the other side of the church, showing a lord of the manor of Acton just 420 years later, and in such a different tradition of English art? At Belton, Lincs, the memorial to Sir John Brownlow, 1697, mentions that he was the builder of the house, and Katharine Esdaile attributed this monument to William Stanton who was master mason there. At Shepshed, Leics, there is a series of memorials to members of the Phillipps family who lived at Garendon, one of whom was a lawyer who, in the words of the inscription on his monument, 'retired to the country where he made himself useful by composing differences and preventing lawsuits amongst his neighbours, and spent much of his time building, planting and other improvements'. For a lawyer in retirement, what occupation could be better than preventing lawsuits? Other members of the family rebuilt the house and added to the landscape of Garendon by building an obelisk, temple and gateway which still survive, although the house itself, after being altered in Victorian times, was eventually destroyed and the materials used as hardcore for the motorway which runs through the estate.

The M1 motorway, which passes Garendon and cuts through

the rocky outcrops of Charnwood Forest, continues northward across the Trent and into the industrial area on the Derbyshire–Nottinghamshire border, a dreary landscape of ironworks and collieries with little interest to the motorist until, in the Chester-field area, something quite remarkable happens. The observant passenger will notice a wooded ridge rising to the east of the motorway and on it, if conditions are favourable, he may see two of the most dramatic buildings in the Midlands. In a bright western light these buildings have a magic that is enhanced by their contrasting moods. Hardwick Hall is square and solemn, dark grey and dark brown, with strange towers that seem to re-group themselves as one travels on, at one moment separated by spaces of sky but at another moment closing together. Bolsover Castle, at the northern end of the same ridge, seems to be silvery white, a fantasy of unfamiliar shapes, like stage scenery left behind after the masques produced for royal entertainment, which is exactly what this place is. Then from a different age, as classical as the others are romantic, the ruined mansion of Sutton Scarsdale can be picked out on the other side of the motorway, facing Hardwick and Bolsover. This un-expected piece of noble landscape, so unlike that seen from that other motorway at Croome, is even better represented by monuments, for this is Cavendish country and the monuments of these landscape-makers and their connections are not in one place but scattered far and wide from Sheffield to Westminster.

Everyone has heard of Bess of Hardwick, that formidable character of Queen Elizabeth's time (p 53), who devoted so much of her vast fortune to building projects in her native Derbyshire, but not everyone is aware that we can come face to face with her on her monument in Derby Cathedral (p 53) and read there a contemporary record of her activities: 'This very celebrated Elizabeth Countess of Shrewsbury built the houses of Chatsworth, Hardwick and Oldcotes, highly distin-guished by their magnificence . . .' Of these, only Hardwick remains as she knew it, for the old Chatsworth which was built when she was married to Sir William Cavendish assumed its present form of a ducal palace more than a century later, and the site of Oldcotes is now a farm. So Hardwick Hall and the great coloured monument of its builder are both important, not only because of Bess but because they represent a whole era of our history, the powerful families of the north Midlands, the court of Elizabeth and the intrigues in connection with Mary Queen of Scots, as well as those concerning the grand-daughter of Bess, the unhappy Arabella Stuart, and her possible accession to the throne. The monument also mentions Bess's four husbands and her sons and daughters, these names introducing us to other buildings and other monuments. Her son William, who became Earl of Devonshire, and founded that branch of the family, with a later dukedom, shares an elaborate memorial with his brother Henry at Edensor, the model village at the gates of Chatsworth, while Charles whose descendants became dukes of Newcastle was the builder of much of Bolsover Castle and has his monument in the church there. Bess's fourth husband, George Talbot, 6th Earl of Shrewsbury, died at Sheffield at one of his houses where Mary Queen of Scots had been held in captivity, but by then he had quarrelled with Bess, and his monument in Sheffield Cathedral does not even mention her name. If we look further afield we shall find others that do mention her, but it is time to turn from the patrons of builders and craftsmen to the men themselves who played their part in establishing the traditions of Elizabethan and Jacobean England.

In his important book on Robert Smythson, Mark Girouard reveals the role played by the Smythson family in contributing, either directly or indirectly, to so many of the great houses being erected in this country during the late sixteenth and early seventeenth centuries. Here again we shall find that memorials help us to visualise these men to whom we owe cherished elements in the landscape today. Just over a hundred years before Wren's famous epitaph was placed in the crypt of St Paul's Cathedral, a memorial tablet was put up in the church at Wollaton, close to Nottingham, to commemorate Robert Smythson, one of the first men that we can call 'architect' in an age when individual designers were becoming more easily distinguished from masons. The inscription describes him as 'architector and survayor unto the most worthy house of Wollaton with diverse others of great account'. It would have been nice if the houses could have been more exactly specified, but fortunately there are records telling us that Smythson was employed at Longleat, Wardour and Hardwick, buildings which were indeed of 'great account'. Moreover, the influence of his family extended to many more in the northern counties. Architects and craftsmen of repute must have been in great demand in later sixteenth-century England when the spoils of the monasteries were enriching so many of the influential families, so we hear of Smythson working for Sir John Thynne at Longleat from 1568 onwards, and for Sir Matthew Arundell at Wardour in 1576. By 1580 he was building Wollaton for the cousin and brother-in-law of Arundell, Sir Francis Willoughby, and on this project there were craftsmen who had worked at Longleat and Chatsworth, and who were to appear later at Hardwick.[9]

Hardwick was built between 1590 and 1597, and on her way north from London in 1592 Bess called on her daughter Frances who was married to Sir Henry Pierrepont.[10] Amongst the gilded strapwork of Sir Henry's monument in the church at Holme Pierrepont, near Nottingham, we find a reference to the fact that 'Ladie Frances was the eldest daughter of Sir William Cavendish of Chatsworth, knight, and the most noble and renowned Ladie Elizabeth his wife, late Countesse of Shrewsbury'. From Holme Pierrepont, Bess journeyed to the other side of Nottingham to visit her friend Sir Francis Willoughby in that stylish new house of his, which must have been of special interest to her at that moment when her own work at Hardwick was still in its early stages. There is only one small reference to Smythson being paid for work at Hardwick,[11] so perhaps Bess controlled the design herself, as may have been the case with

Cecil at Burghley and perhaps Thynne at Longleat. Bess may even have borrowed him while he was employed on his Cavendish and Talbot commissions in the north, in the same way that her husband had earlier tried, without success, to borrow a Longleat plasterer for work at Chatsworth. By the time Bess's son and grandson were undertaking their own building programmes at Bolsover, so near to Hardwick, it was the younger Smythsons who were involved, first John and then Huntingdon, who spent most of their lives working on those fanciful buildings that deliberately recall the former days of tournaments and chivalry and which made a splendid setting for Ben Jonson's masque at the visit of Charles I. If we search for the Smythson memorials at Bolsover church we find these lines written for Huntingdon Smythson, who died in 1648, his career brought to an end by insanity, and the Civil War:

> Reader beneath this plaine stone ly
> Smithson's remainders of mortality
> Whose skill at architecture did deserve
> A fairer tombe his memr'y to preserve . . .[12]

We have devoted considerable time to this part of Derbyshire because there is no better place for demonstrating the way in which monuments reflect the personalities behind the builders and the landscape-makers. We may end this section with a final glimpse that summarises this corner of 'Cavendish Country', and take the narrow lanes to the village of Ault Hucknall. If we stand in the churchyard and look to north and south we can see Bolsover on the one side and Hardwick on the other, and then inside the impressive Norman church we must look for three things that are relevant to our story. There is a most unusual monument to the 1st Countess of Devonshire, linking this place with the Chatsworth branch of the family; near it is the floorstone to Thomas Hobbes, the philosopher, who died at Hardwick at the age of ninety-one after serving two earls of Devonshire; and finally there is a tablet with a delightful verse to Robert Hackett, keeper of Hardwick Park. So countess, philosopher and gamekeeper lie in the same church, that same church that was used for a lookout-post when Bess's son Henry Cavendish, with forty armed men, attempted to abduct Arabella from her grandmother's custody at Hardwick and make her the future Queen of England.

LANDSCAPE GARDENERS

Throughout all the counties of England where great parklands clothe and beautify the landscape there are monuments to the landowners who planted the trees that have since grown to maturity. In general, the planting was formal with straight avenues and long vistas during late Stuart and early Georgian times, and one thinks of the peers who enriched the countryside around Badminton and Cirencester, Boughton and Holkham, each of whom has a monument in the appropriate church. The appropriate church is not always the one you think it is, so in a later chapter we shall consider this aspect of our study. During the latter half of the eighteenth century when landscaping became informal we continue to find memorials to those who created this type of parkland, although the actual mention of these projects, such as we found at Croome, is still of rare occurrence. There must be many more to be discovered, particularly amongst those rather tiresome Latin inscriptions which are too lengthy and too full of praise, and which one therefore tends to neglect. However, there are some of special interest which are concerned either with patrons or the actual landscape designers, and these are always worth finding.

At Scraptoft, near Leicester, the monument to James Wigley is perhaps unique in having a delightful little relief showing the owner of Scraptoft Hall, in a three-cornered hat, supervising the planting of trees on the estate. As at Croome, the work was carried out with an eye to providing useful occupation for the poor. Much of this landscape remains, for the setting was care-fully preserved, as far as was possible, when the hall was extended to form a College of Education, so there are still glades and groves with a mound that conceals the remains of a grotto, though the pretty little summer house that once stood on its summit has gone. As early as the 1780s the historian Throsby was describing Scraptoft groves as:

> . . . a treat to Leicester people of all descriptions. Hither the chaise, the chair and the horse, loaded with visitants . . . come to traverse the shady walks . . . In them, lovers cherish the fond hope, foster the deep-fetch'd sigh and see, or think they see, bliss await them . . .[13]

James Wigley was MP for Leicester and there is a fine portrait of him, by Joseph Highmore, in the City Art Gallery. It is interesting to compare this with the portrait busts of his parents on their monument in the church that stands so beautifully alongside Scraptoft Hall, presumably the house built for the father, Sir Edward Wigley, and still preserving a spacious fore-court with a very grand set of wrought-iron gates. Long may the encroaching tide of suburbia be prevented from engulfing this place, where the memorials of landscape-makers so clearly reveal the eighteenth-century personalities behind the scene.

During the Midland tour in 1789 that took the Hon John Byng to Grimsthorpe he also visited Wrest Park in Bedfordshire and in his customary disparaging manner he had nothing good to say of the house or of the cooking at the local inn, though he was pleased with his brown bread and sage cheese. He was critical, too, when he went to the church at Flitton, two miles away,

> to view the monuments of the Kent family who here show in marble magnificence. The old recumbent Figures of Henry Erle of Kent, and his Countess, are very fine; but those of a later date are abominable: a Son of the last Duke, a Lad in a Wig and Shirt! The Duke himself, upon a cumb'rous Monument, as a Roman, with his English Ducal Cap![14]

Even today many will still prefer the earlier monument, for it comes from that excellent school of sculpture that flourished in the reign of Charles I, although this example was not erected until 1658. What concerns us now is the inscription beneath the large figure of the 1st Duke of Kent (p 54), the one that was so distasteful to Byng, for it was this de Grey who established the gardens at Wrest Park and built the town house of the family, as his epitaph tells us:

> His taste and magnificence are still conspicuous in the elegant house which he erected for the Town residence of his family and in the Beautiful and spacious Gardens which he laid out and finished at his favourite seat in this neighbourhood.

He also remodelled the old house at Wrest, now replaced by the present mansion in the French style, occupied by the National Institute of Agricultural Engineering. Part of the park is open during the summer, so we can enjoy the radiating walks, a number of attractive garden buildings and the celebrated Long Water leading to Thomas Archer's pavilion. How fortunate that this layout of the early period survives, for opinions change as regards gardens as well as monuments. Just as the duke's figure, which annoyed Byng, may now be better appreciated in our day, so the duke's gardens which to us seem a treasured survival were considered to be in very bad taste by late eighteenth-century standards. When Horace Walpole visited Wrest Park he described the grounds as

> . . . ugly in the old fashioned manner with high hedges and canals, at the End of the principal one of which there is a frightful Temple designed by Mr. Archer, the groomporter. Mr. Brown has much corrected this garden and built a hermitage and cold bath in bold good taste.[15]

At this time Lancelot Brown was employing his astonishing

skill and vision to 'correct' a great many gardens, and no individual has ever had such a far-reaching effect on the landscape of England. Dorothy Stroud's biography of Brown provides a most absorbing account of his undertakings in park after park, transforming the rigid geometry of avenues and formal gardens into a 'natural' scene in which straight canals became curving lakes and open grassland swept right up to the windows of the house. We have already seen at Grimsthorpe and Croome that one main vista was usually retained, and we feel grateful for this when we see Blenheim and Castle Ashby, Hampton Court, Chillington, Corsham and others where he spared the noble trees of the grand approach, even when his patrons wanted the rest of the park 'corrected' and brought into line with 'bold good taste'. At Burghley he was employed in architectural work as well as with landscaping and he seems to have been particularly conscious of his own contribution to the splendour of that seat, for he wrote in 1778: 'This is a great place where I have had twenty five years pleasure in restoring the monument of a great minister to a great Queen.'[16]

At Burghley there is still an avenue to the north, but the one to the north-west, shown in an early drawing preserved in the house, was modified to do away with the rows of trees and yet retain the unusual, perhaps unique, vista towards the town of Stamford. Many such vistas aim at a church in the far distance, as a terminal feature, Brown retained one at Castle Ashby that is in alignment with Easton Mandit spire, but what is so unusual about this view from the Pagoda Room at Burghley is that two of the spires of Stamford, St Mary and All Saints, coincide from this angle so that one rises exactly behind the other, in alignment with the house. To add a nice touch to this, it is a pleasure to see that the appropriate window is flanked by a portrait of Lancelot Brown.

Portraits frequently lead us to monuments, and vice versa, so it is time we made the journey to Fenstanton, near Huntingdon, to look for Brown's memorial. We shall find it on the north side of the stately fourteenth-century chancel, a building with lovely

Page 53   (*right*) Elizabeth, Countess of Shrewsbury (Bess of Hardwick)

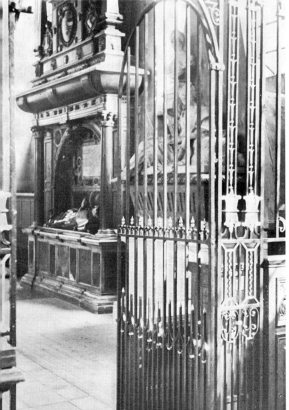

(*left*) Derby Cathedral. The Cavendish chapel with the tomb of Bess of Hardwick, d 1607. The inscription refers to her building projects at Chatsworth, Hardwick and Oldcotes

Page 54 (*left*) Flitton (Beds). Henry de Grey, 1st Duke of Kent. Designed by Edward Shepherd, the figure probably **by** Rysbrack, 1740. The inscription refers **to** the gardens at Wrest Park

(*right*) Stourton (Wilts). Detail of the monument to Henry Hoare the younger, the creator of the gardens at Stourhead. By Charles Harris, 1785

curvilinear windows and the matrix of the founder's brass, but it was the revived Gothic of the eighteenth century that was employed when Lancelot Brown's monument was placed here when he died in 1783. The epitaph bears a reference to his fame as a landscape-maker but rather nicely makes a plea that he should be remembered not only for his genius but also for more homely virtues.

> Ye Sons of Elegance, who truly taste
> The simple charms that genuine Art supplies,
> Come from the sylvan Scenes His Genius grac'd
> And offer here your tributory Sighs.
> But know that more than Genius slumbers here;
> Virtues were his which Art's best powers transcend.
> Come, ye Superior train, who these revere
> And weep the Christian, Husband, Father, Friend.

Another gardener who had considerable influence was William Shenstone, whose grounds at The Leasowes, near Halesowen, were visited by Horace Walpole, Dr Johnson and countless other literary and artistic persons. In the grounds of the golf course that now occupies the site there are some interesting traces, but much has been destroyed; what concerns us here is the fact that in Halesowen church there is a handsome urn upon a pedestal, commemorating Shenstone. At Aylsham church, in Norfolk, outside the chancel, there is a monument to the Repton family which recalls the landscaping activities of Humphry Repton, the self-styled successor to Capability Brown. He, in his turn, 'corrected' several of what he considered the excesses of Brown, and his well-known Red Books demonstrate his methods, the effect of 'before and after' being indicated by ingenious flaps which could be folded back.

There is no better place to finish this survey of monuments and landscape-makers than Stourhead, perhaps the loveliest of all our man-made landscapes, lying amongst the hills where Wiltshire meets both Somerset and Dorset. Since the eighteenth century the grounds at Stourhead have been much praised and admirably described, as well as visited by thousands every year, but our special concern is something that is not always appreciated. When you have made the circuit of the lake and looked with amazement at the grotto where the river god and nymph appear miraculously white amidst the watery gloom, and at the Pantheon with its interior of classical perfection, when you have climbed to the Temple of the Sun and looked down on all the beauty that Henry Hoare established, you can then slip quietly into the church at the entrance to the gardens and find his monument (p 54), then read his epitaph which so elegantly relates the man to his handiwork:

> Ye who have view'd in Pleasure's choicest hour
> The Earth Embellish'd on these Banks of Stour,
> With grateful Reverence to this Marble lean,
> Rais'd to the Friendly Founder of the Scene.
> Here, with pure love of smiling Nature warm'd,
> This far-fam'd Demy-Paradise he form'd:
> And, happier still, here learn'd from Heaven to find
> A sweeter Eden in a Bounteous Mind.
> Thankful these fair and flowery paths he trod,
> And priz'd them only as they lead to God.

So here is another instance of the living landscape as a memorial, but although a demi-paradise is nobler than any epitaph, we would not wish to be without this monument in Stourton church, by that same Charles Harris of London who did the more ambitious composition commemorating the 3rd and 4th Dukes of Ancaster, at Edenham in Lincolnshire. That other memorial that we saw at Croome, with its neo-classical figure mourning by an urn, and its 'look around you' theme in Latin, was cold and formal in comparison with this more genial work at Stourton with two little putti playing around an urn, adorning it with leaves and holding the inscription for all lovers of Stourhead gardens to read, in friendly English.

One of the special delights of Stourhead is to find oneself in the very centre of things, even before entering, on a wide green amidst a very attractive group of buildings. On one side there is an inn that was built for the refreshment of eighteenth-century visitors to the gardens, then comes the church with a smooth greensward sweeping right up to its gates; opposite stands a pretty row of cottages and then, as a sort of centrepiece, rises the slender spire of the medieval cross from the middle of old Bristol. Beyond lies the lake, the bridge, and at the far end of half a mile of glittering water stands the Pantheon, its solemn outline providing a classical answer to the Gothic church and the prickly pinnacles of the Bristol Cross, the ideal realisation of the English gentleman's desire to recreate the art of the painter in terms of landscape.

Close to Henry Hoare's monument in Stourton church there is a larger one to his father, Henry Hoare the elder, for whom Colen Campbell built the house at Stourhead in the 1720s, and the father's bust which tops his monument has the longer wig of that period, for he died soon after the house was built. As one would expect at that date, there were plans to provide Stourhead with formal gardens, but Henry Hoare the younger had other ideas and used to full advantage the natural contours of the site. One has to remember that when this project was first undertaken, in the 1740s, Capability Brown was still an almost unknown assistant working under William Kent at Stowe in Buckinghamshire, where happily the grandeur of the grounds still survives to form one of the few rivals to Stourhead, so Hoare's enterprise was an early example of the change in taste, and one that avoids the 'shaven and shorn' appearance for which many of Brown's schemes were later criticised.

Unlike Croome, Grimsthorpe and Wrest, where we have already linked landscapes with monuments, but where the houses are not normally open, Stourhead is the property of the National Trust and there is regular public access, affording an excellent opportunity to relate portraits and furniture to the men and their landscape. In the entrance hall there is a large equestrian portrait of Henry Hoare the younger, the figure by Dahl but the horse by Wootton, and near it hang paintings of Henry Hoare the elder, holding an architect's drawing of the new house, and Richard Colt Hoare, the grandson of the young Hoare who planted the grounds. Richard Colt Hoare was the historian of Wiltshire and a great antiquary; he added the wings to Stourhead to contain his famous library and picture gallery. From the point of view of our present study it is interesting to see, in the gallery, paintings by Claude, the Poussins and others that clearly indicate the type of ideal classical landscape, with temples standing by water, which so profoundly influenced Hoare in the planning of Stourhead gardens. In the library there is Rysbrack's terracotta model for his figure of Hercules which stands in the Pantheon, by the lake, also a small replica of Chantrey's monument to Richard Colt Hoare in Salisbury Cathedral.

The pillared front of Stourhead looks eastward towards the high chalk outposts of Salisbury Plain; it seems to turn its back on the gardens as if determined to have nothing whatever to do with the picturesque mood of a later generation. But if we descend from the lawn behind the house, which leads rather formally to an obelisk, we drop steeply to the lush valley of woods and water, with temples mirrored in the lake, and we can experience something of the change that was brought about by the younger Hoare. His landscape has, of course, matured since his day but from eighteenth-century prints and the writings of visitors such as Horace Walpole it is clear that by the time forty years had elapsed, and the monument to Hoare was erected in 1785, the 'friendly founder of the scene' had been able to look with satisfaction on his 'far-famed demi-paradise' and see that it was good.

Chapter 3

HISTORY ENGRAVED

. . . so eminently loyal in hazarding both his life and fortune
by concealing in his house the most sacred person of our late
most Gracious Sovereign King Charles the Second till he
could provide means for his escape into France.

From the monument to Sir George Norton,
Abbots Leigh, Avon

An episode in history, such as the escape of Charles II after the
battle of Worcester, becomes so real when we find the evidence
on memorials, and each inscription reads like a press report,
preserving a contemporary record that brings history to life
and makes it seem like the day before yesterday. All along the
route from the famous oak tree at Boscabel to the harbour at
Shoreham in Sussex there were Royalist friends who helped
the fugitive king, hiding him in their houses, providing horses
and accompanying Charles when he was disguised as a servant,
but keeping their secret until after the Restoration when it was
safe to reveal family loyalties. Then, when the time came for
monuments to be made for these friends who planned the
king's escape, their part in the story was placed on record,
along with the honours bestowed by a grateful monarch.

The Giffards, whose chief seat was at Chillington in Staffordshire, were influential in finding shelter for Charles, first at
Whiteladies and then at Boscabel, two Giffard properties close
together on the Shropshire–Staffordshire border between Tong
and Brewood. Boscabel House is still in deep country and there
you can see the secret chambers and the garden house which

59

will forever be associated with the king's stay there, under the care of the Penderels. The oak tree across the fields is protected by a railing which bears an inscription, but whether this is the actual tree, or a descendant, we must leave to the experts; what we do know is that while hiding in the branches Charles was supported and provided with food by Major Carlis, or Carlos, who was eventually rewarded with a grant of arms as well as the proceeds of a tax on all hay and straw taken into London and Westminster. There is a memorial to Carlis in the church at Brewood and a helpful translation of the actual grant of the coat of arms, which incorporated an oak tree, but the chief glory of this church is the noble series of Giffard monuments, of coloured alabaster on both sides of the chancel, showing the subtle changes in armour and head-dress from Henry VIII to Charles I. There are ten adult figures and no less than forty-nine children.

The subsequent wanderings of Charles are well known, especially the journey he made after being concealed at Moseley Old Hall, when, disguised as a servant and riding pillion with Jane Lane of Bentley, he arrived at Abbots Leigh near Bristol. It was here that he was concealed by Sir George Norton whose monument in the church bears the reference quoted at the opening of this chapter, but we scarcely expect the Norton family's declaration of loyalty to be spread as far as a cousin, whose memorial in Bath Abbey mentions the distinction achieved by the house of his relative at Abbots Leigh. An unexpected reference to the part played by the Lanes of Bentley can be seen at Manningford Bruce in Wiltshire where, in an early Norman church, there is a memorial to Mary, the sister of the better-known Jane, from which it appears that both women played a prominent part in the king's escape.

Underneath lieth the body of Mary Nicholas, daughter of Thomas Lane of Bentley, in the county of Stafford, esquire, a family as venerable for its antiquity as renowned for its loyalty, of which the wonderful preservation of King Charles the Second after the defeat at Worcester is an instance never to be forgotten, in which glorious action she herself bore a considerable part, and that the memory of this extraordinary service might be continued to posterity, the family was dignified with the addition of this signal badge of honour: the arms of England in a canton. She was married to Edward Nicholas, the son of Sir Oliver Nicholas, cupbearer to King James the First and carver to King Charles the First . . .

The king's hiding-place at Trent, near Sherborne in Dorset, where he finally parted with Jane Lane, was to become an important point in this dramatic journey, for his proposed embarkation at Charmouth was planned from here, and when this attempt failed he returned to Trent before setting out for Heale House, near Salisbury, and so eventually to the coast. The church at Trent stands in a setting of great beauty, for the village is of silver-grey stone set amongst the loveliest of trees and the greenest of lawns, with parkland backed by wooded hills. The churchyard is bordered by a choice group of buildings, the almshouses, the chantry, and the manor house where Charles was concealed, and the church contains, amongst many other treasures, monuments to the Gerards and the Wyndhams who owned the manor. The memorial to the younger Sir Francis Wyndham bears a reference to his father's part in the king's escape, as well as his ultimate reward.

He was the third son of Sir Francis Wyndham of this place, who in consideration of his constant and faithful services to King Charles the First and Second, in quality of a lieutenant-colonel of horse, but more particularly for his being instrumental in preserving King Charles the Second in his house here, after the unfortunate Battle of Worcester, till his retreat to France, was by him soon after his restoration created a baronet, with a large pension to attend the honour, as a farther token of his royal favour.

Trent church has monuments from the fourteenth to the

nineteenth centuries, one of which, to Anne Gerard, 1633, must surely be unique, for it is incorporated into an arch which bears a complex family tree with more than forty shields amongst painted branches, and there is a strange inscription with reversed lettering which doesn't seem to read properly whichever way you look at it. The woodwork of screen, pulpit and benches is quite spectacular in its richness and there is some memorable glass.

A part of the inscription on Sir Francis Wyndham's memorial at Trent, previous to the lines quoted above, refers to the origins of the family at the village of Felbrigg in Norfolk, reminding us of the far-flung ramifications of this study of monuments. At Felbrigg there is a wonderful series of brasses and tablets commemorating first the Felbriggs and then the Wyndhams. Felbrigg Hall was built by the latter family, whose brasses mention their other property at Orchard Wyndham, near Watchet in Somerset. If we go to Watchet and climb to the church of St Decumen, a fine building in an isolated setting, high on the hill behind the little seaport, we shall find, behind the family pew, another series of Wyndham brasses and monuments, which, in their turn, mention Felbrigg. One of them bears a nice example of the way in which the Civil War was referred to in later years: 'Sir William Wyndham of Orchard Wyndham . . . of the noble family of Wyndham of Felbrigg . . . devoted himself to the closing of the dreadful breach of the late monstrous divisions.' Their seat at Kentsford, close to St Decumen's church, is also referred to on these memorials and there are marriage links with the Wadhams of Merrifield, with whom we shall be concerned later, the Trevelyans of Nettlecombe and that branch of the Wyndham family that took the title of Egremont, at Petworth. A floorstone to Sir Hugh Wyndham, 1671, has yet another reference to the Civil War.

Here lies beneath this ragged stone
One more his Princes than his owne
And in his marterd Father's Warrs
Lost fortune, blood, gained naught but scarrs . . .

Monuments that mention the Civil War are to be found all over the country and the inscriptions are always worth reading, if only to discover the political allegiance of the person commemorated. If the memorial was erected before the Restoration the terms used to describe the conflict may be more guarded than those of a later date when the clouds of uncertainty had cleared. At Holme Pierrepont, near Nottingham, a certain Princess Gertrude is described on a monument of 1649 as having been married to one of the generals to Charles I, 'in the late unhappy differences'; but at Edenham, where we have already seen such fine Bertie monuments, the 2nd Earl of Lindsey who died in 1666 is described as being 'present at the funeral of Charles I, amid the very cruelty of the mad tyrant: he followed his king to his grave, greatly daring to condemn the rebels by his own devotion'. At the battle of Edgehill he had 'with his own body protected the general, his father, who lay prostrate and mortally wounded'. After all this it is satisfactory to learn that after following the king's coffin to Windsor from Whitehall the earl eventually became one of the court that tried the regicides. An example from the opposite camp occurs at Caldecote, near Nuneaton, where Colonel Purefoy was one of the commissioners at the trial of Charles I and a signatory to the death warrant. In this case he died in 1659, just before the Restoration and just in time, politically speaking, for a regicide. In the dark chancel of the little church that stands in the grounds of Caldecote Hall there is a tablet that tells the story of the defence of Purefoy's house, in the absence of the colonel, by his son-in-law George Abbott, whose monument records the episode from the Parliamentarian point of view as a 'memorable and unparralelled defence of the adjoining house with 8 men, beside

63

his mother and her maids, against the furious assault of Prince Rupert and Maurice with 18 Troops of Horse and dragoons . . .'

Another instance of the Parliamentary side being represented on a monument is at Noseley in Leicestershire, the seat of the Hazleriggs, where the private chapel stands in the grounds of the hall and is approached by a long drive through the woods. This is a beautiful setting, best seen when the grounds are open because of the daffodils, when the chapel seems to stand ankle-deep in green and gold, or when, on a warm summer night, there is a concert here and lights sparkle to make the whole place come to life. The floor is paved with incised slabs bearing the figures of Hazlerigg knights, and along the walls the gilded heraldry of the Renaissance catches the same dancing light that is reflected from cello and violin, oboe and flute. There is an important monument to Sir Arthur Hazlerigg, one of the out-standing political figures during the Commonwealth, a staunch puritan who opposed every attempt to set up any authority other than Parliament. He was governor of Newcastle and a member of every council of state during the Commonwealth, yet he was constantly at loggerheads with Cromwell, the govern-ment and the army, and opposed the recognition of Richard Cromwell as the new Protector. At the Restoration he was flung into the Tower and died, as his epitaph puts it, 'in England's peaceable year 1660', and he is described as one 'who enjoyed his portion of this life in the times of greatest civil trouble that ever this nation had'.

In a later chapter we shall be considering memorials that show a person twice in the same church, first as a child and again on his own monument, but while we are at Noseley it will be well to note a good example of this. Only a few feet to the west of Sir Arthur Hazlerigg's tomb there is a richly coloured one of his parents, and amongst the eight sons and six daughters the future Parliamentarian kneels at the front of the line of boys. Here there is a human touch that makes this splendid piece of costume and heraldry particularly interesting, for when we have admired the figures of Sir Thomas and Dame Frances his wife, and the intricate detailing of the little children, we read that the mother 'adorned her family with fine cloth of her own spinning'.

Also in Leicestershire, but on the other side of the county at Stoke Golding, there is an inscription which gives us another glimpse of contemporary attitudes, not only to the Civil War but also to the events that followed. This time we are on the Royalist side and the memorial to Henry Firebrace has a most unusual reference to the 'departure' of Charles II and James II, under very different circumstances, and to the board that controlled the accounts within the royal household. It is worth quoting at some length in terms of a free translation of the original Latin.

> . . . after the arms of rebels were victorious and tyranny imposed upon us, he retired to the country, near this village, until, Heaven looking graciously upon the hopes of all men, Charles who was missed so much, returned to his own land.
>
> Then he [Henry Firebrace] discharged honourable duties, without peril, in the Royal Household where he took control of private household affairs among the principal officials of the Green Cloth, as people call it, enjoying now a more happy fortune.
>
> With such integrity he lived for nearly 30 years at court . . . and because of his incorruptibility he was ever dear to Charles and James, those august brothers. The one yielded to Nature, the other to Fortune, and eventually the court was disbanded. In order to keep faith he returned to this familiar haven and former refuge.

So we gather that the Royalist sympathies of Henry Firebrace drove him to retreat to Stoke Golding and then his Jacobite loyalties led him to return once again to this village on the advent of William of Orange. This is an example of one of those long Latin inscriptions that prove daunting to all but the most determined 'monument hunters', yet are found to be so worth while. Stoke Golding church is locally renowned for its distinguished fourteenth-century architecture, but only the rare enthusiast will discover that the rather ordinary memorial in an obscure corner reveals the story of a Stuart court official.

Before we leave Leicestershire we must visit Wistow where the hall stands by the edge of a lake, and on the other side of the road a leafy lane through a spinney takes us to the church which stands by the river, and a footbridge leads to a green expanse of water meadows. It was at Wistow that Charles I and Prince Rupert stayed at the time of the battle of Naseby, for the house of the Halfords was a local centre for the Royalist cause. After the disaster of Naseby the royal party fled in haste to Leicester, leaving their saddles and equipment at Wistow, to be called for at a more convenient time, and there Sir Richard Halford kept these precious things for the king who never returned. Those who came after have guarded them carefully and the two saddles covered in richly embroidered red velvet can still be seen at Wistow, with swords and pistols, and gilded stirrups with blue enamelled decoration. We know why the king never came back for his saddles and arms, indeed Sir Richard Halford himself narrowly escaped execution at the hands of Cromwell because his son hanged some Roundheads after a skirmish in this valley. Sir Richard died just before the Restoration and his monument was set up in Wistow church; it is in the north transept behind some handsome wrought-iron gates which date from the following century when both church and house were given a new look. Similar ironwork, painted white, makes a delicate lace-like pattern in front of the dark oak of the Georgian reredos, and there are royal arms, a Halford hatchment and box pews with rows of little hat pegs.

Later Halfords have mural tablets in the church at Wistow, and one of them is of special interest because of a strange sequel to this story. A relative named Henry Vaughan, who succeeded to the estate and then took the name of Halford, became Royal Physician to George III, George IV and William IV, and by one of those delightful coincidences of history this guardian of the king's saddles also became the guardian of one of the king's severed neck-bones. It came about in the year 1813 when some excavations were being made at St George's Chapel, Windsor. Close to the coffin of Henry VIII in the royal vault there was an unidentified one which was thought to be that of Charles, taken there after the execution at Whitehall, accompanied by a few loyal supporters including Montagu Bertie, 2nd Earl of Lindsey, whose monument we have seen at Edenham. The Prince Regent ordered the nameless coffin to be examined, and Sir Henry Halford of Wistow, as Royal Physician, was present. When proof had been established and the body with its severed head had been replaced and the coffin sealed, it was found that a fragment of the fractured neck had not been put back with the rest. The Prince Regent then gave the bone to his physician for safe-keeping, and so in some measure, at least, the king returned to Wistow to rest with the saddles and arms that were left here 168 years before, and here the royal bone remained until it was returned to the dark vault at Windsor in 1888.

THE COMMONWEALTH RECALLED

There are several monuments which were erected a long time after the Civil War yet bear some reference to it, and typical of these is the one at Maiden Bradley, in Wiltshire, to Sir Edward Seymour, Bt, Speaker of the House of Commons. He died in 1707 but Rysbrack's splendid figure of the baronet was not set up until 1730, and the inscription is of interest because it makes reference to the Civil War and the Restoration, although both were so far removed from the reign of George II when the monument was made.

His childhood felt not the calamities which in the succeeding years the spirit of anarchy and schism spread over the nation. His manhood saw the church and monarchy restored.

67

This Seymour memorial recalls the vast extent of that family's estates, stretching from Devon to London, for Sir Edward is styled 'late of Berry Pomeroy'. It is at that village that we can begin the long journey from the Dart to the Thames, finding Seymour houses and Seymour monuments all the way. At Maiden Bradley the tablets and floorstones that commemorate members of the family remind us that the Georgian house just beyond the churchyard wall is the seat of the present Duke of Somerset and it is visible through the plain glass of the east window, in the chancel which is so beautifully furnished in a restrained modern manner. Maiden Bradley church has many other delights including a complete set of very fine seventeenth-century pews in commemoration of the Restoration, a copy of the alabaster tablet at Great Bedwyn which records the Seymour history, and a beautifully lettered floorstone from modern times which lists ten members of the ducal family buried here. One of the Victorian mural monuments is worth a close look because it shows the earlier spelling of the family name, St Maur, and commemorates two sons of the 12th Duke of Somerset, one of whom died under Garibaldi, 'fighting in the cause of Italy's freedom', and the other who was 'accidentally wounded by a bear' while shooting in India. Maiden Bradley lies half-way between Longleat and Stourhead in the rolling green landscape of Salisbury Plain, but in contrast to the open chalklands all around, the village is hidden in enormous trees and from the cool interior of the church you can hear birdsong in Bradley Park, accompanied by that other lovely summer sound, somebody else using a mower, and in this case it is on the ducal lawn.

Another example of retrospective references occurs at Brightwell Baldwin in Oxfordshire where, in the north aisle of the church, there stands one of those surprising 'multiple monuments', in which several members of one family are commemorated by a series of white urns in dark niches. The whole thing must look rather eerie if you are in the church at dusk, but no more so than those other collective memorials which have solemn tiers of busts, one above the other, like those at Edenham, Lincolnshire, and Stapleford, Leicestershire. This idea is seen again at Blockley in Gloucestershire, where, above the raised family vault, the Rushouts of Northwick Park have a series of busts, some of which are signed by Rysbrack. The urns at Brightwell Baldwin make a very impressive display going right up to the roof and are in memory of the Stone family. From the inscription it appears that it was the Fire of London, as well as the Civil War, that led to this 'family gathering' in this pleasant village between Oxford and the Chilterns.

> . . . the trouble following the father's, and the Fire of London succeeding the son's death, this memorial of their graves (not to be found after that dismal conflagration) is transmitted with their family to this place.

Of all the retrospective memorials the most remarkable is that of Chaloner Chute, Speaker of the House of Commons at the end of the Commonwealth period. Like Colonel Purefoy at Caldecote and Sir Richard Halford of Wistow, he died just before the Restoration. Chute's epitaph has a very interesting comment on those hazardous times:

> . . . Speaker of the House of Commons in the Parliament of Richard Cromwell when amidst the various and struggling interests of that complicated year, to the regret of all parties he died in the service of his arduous post, 14 April 1659.

But the most astonishing aspects of this monument to Chaloner Chute are its date and its location. It was not designed until 1775, more than a century after his death, and it is not in a church but in a tomb chamber attached to the private chapel at The Vyne, near Basingstoke. In earlier times The Vyne was the home of William Sandys, Lord Chamberlain to Henry VIII, and much of this early Tudor house remains, including the lovely chapel with contemporary glass. The Civil War impoverished the Sandys family, and The Vyne was sold to Chaloner Chute who made several alterations including the striking white portico on the garden front, at that time an innovation and introduced here in 1654 by John Webb whom we met at Wilton where he completed the work of Inigo Jones. Webb's master mason at The Vyne was Edward Marshall, a sculptor who executed some of the fireplaces, the Chute coat of arms on the portico and, elsewhere in the country, some notable monuments. Edward Marshall became master mason to the Crown at the Restoration, and was succeeded in that office by his son Joshua with whom we shall be concerned later.

It was John Chute, the Speaker's great-grandson, who inherited the estate in 1754 and made further alterations to The Vyne. He was a close friend of Horace Walpole, so we are not surprised to find parts of the house in a 'Strawberry Hill Gothick' style. Indeed, Chute had plans for Gothicising the whole place, as we can see in the portrait of him by Gabriel Mathias in the Further Drawing Room, in which he is shown holding a drawing of his elaborate project. Horace Walpole said of him:

> Mr. Chute and I agreed invariably in our principles; he was my counsel in my affairs, was my oracle in taste, the standard to whom I submitted my trifles and the genius that presided over poor Strawberry! . . .
> We passed many hours together without saying a syllable to each other, for we were both above ceremony . . . Half is gone, the other remains solitary . . . to me he was the most faithful and secure of friends . . .[1]

The two friends, with other members of 'The Strawberry Committee', had the genuine late Gothic chapel at The Vyne as a precedent for their embellishment of the adjoining rooms, though oddly enough the tomb chamber in 'Strawberry Hill Gothick' contains a classical monument in striking contrast to its setting. For this noble memorial to his ancestor, John Chute designed the sarcophagus, but the reclining figure is a work of

Page 71 (*right*) The Vyne (Hants).
Looking through from the chapel to the
tomb chamber and the monument to
Chaloner Chute, by Thomas Carter,
1775–6

(*below*) Framlingham (Suffolk). Thomas
Howard, 3rd Duke of Norfolk, d 1554.
One of the splendid series of Howard
tombs established here after the
destruction of Thetford Priory

THE RIGHT HONORABLE & NOBLE L
OF RVTLANDE LORD ROSSE OF H.
& BELVOYRE LIETH HERE BVRIED
HIS BROTHER EDWARD IN HIS S.
AND BARONNIES AND THERIN
SATTERDAY THE 24 DAY OF FEBRV
FOLLOWINGE IN THE SAME YEARE
DAY HE DECEASED AT NOTTINGH
HIS CORPS WAS HITHER BROVG
ON THE 2 DAY OF APRILL FOLL

Page 72 (*above*) Titchfield (Hants). The Wriothesley monument by Gerard Johnson, c 1594. Erected in the time of the 3rd Earl of Southampton who was Shakespeare's patron

(*right*) Bottesford (Leics). Detail of the monument to John Manners, 4th Earl of Rutland, by Gerard Johnson. Erected in 1591 after being taken by sea from Southwark to Boston and then in cartloads to Bottesford

incredible dignity by a little-known sculptor named Thomas Carter. This was carried out between the years 1775 and 1776 and is described by Rupert Gunnis as 'one of the noblest works of late eighteenth century sculpture in England', and he gives some interesting details concerning this important work. John Chute died before it was completed so Carter's later bills were sent to his successor at The Vyne and they included items for packing and carriage of the figure from the sculptor's yard in Piccadilly, for loading into a barge and carrying the cases to the wharf; an early instance of canal transport, so clearly suitable for large works of art. The total cost of this splendid monument, together with the marble paving of the tomb chamber, was £930 17s 9d, an enormous sum in eighteenth-century values.[2]

In the monumental art of England there can be few sights more moving than this tomb of Chaloner Chute in its incomparable setting. From the warmth and richness of the Chapel Parlour we pass through to the Ante-Chapel with its 'Gothick' decoration, and then on into the Chapel itself, rather dark on account of its original glass in gorgeous colours showing figures of Henry VIII, Catherine of Aragon and Margaret of Scotland with their patron saints. Along each side are exquisitely carved stalls with canopies and poppy-heads, some of the ornament showing the Renaissance motifs that were just beginning to appear in late Gothic design. Then the climax comes when we pass through from the jewelled twilight of the chapel to the lightness of the tomb-chamber, a more confined space but lit by huge windows, and empty save for the great white monument at its centre (p 71).

Another significant feature of the Chaloner Chute monument is that he is shown in the dress of his own time when he was Speaker, with square-toed shoes, and with a broad-brimmed hat beside him. In 1776 enough was known of the history of costume to ensure that the figure of an illustrious ancestor could be reasonably accurately dressed, but this sort of antiquarianism was rare. For the greater part of the eighteenth century even the

E

dress of their own day was shunned by monumental sculptors in favour of the timeless classicism of ancient Rome, and in such a retrospective work as the Chute figure we should normally find a justifiable resort to the classical mode in costume. Moreover, the Speaker is not gesticulating, or proudly pointing to symbols of his office, nor is he making any of the formal gestures that we so often see in eighteenth-century monuments and which sometimes make them look rather ridiculous. Chaloner Chute is relaxed and silently contemplative, with an ease of manner that adds much to the atmosphere that one feels in that remarkable chapel at The Vyne.

Works of art of the quality of the Chute figure possess a wonderful power of recalling the times in which they were made, extinguishing the years that have elapsed and providing an answer to the query implied in the lines from Gray's 'Elegy', with which we started. They make us ask ourselves what else was being done at that time; who was living then, and what else was happening in the arts? Although the sculptor Thomas Carter is a name known only to a few, there were plenty of better-known men who, in 1776, were at the height of their profession. Gainsborough was 49 and had moved from Bath to London; those three friends, Reynolds, Garrick and Dr Johnson, were 53, 59 and 67 respectively and it was the year of Garrick's last stage appearance, after which he sold part of his share in Drury Lane to Sheridan who had produced *The Rivals* in the previous year, the year that saw the birth of Turner. Horace Walpole was 59 when his friend John Chute died in 1776; Robert Adam was 48, while Lancelot Brown, whom we met as Adam's collaborator at Croome, was 60 and in the midst of his busiest years, transforming the landscape of the aristocracy in several counties at the same time. In that year Mozart was 20 and Haydn 44, and if we consider the foundation then being laid for the future, Constable was born, and Wordsworth and Beethoven were little boys of 6.

HOWARD, WRIOTHESLEY AND MANNERS

Just as the dramatic episodes of the Civil War are brought to life when we discover monuments to the people who were deeply involved in the politics of those times, so it is with the events of a hundred years earlier when the religious and political upheavals of the Reformation were dividing the country and separating the Crown from the papal authority of the Church of Rome. The dissolution of the monasteries led to the aggrandisement of several families so that their monuments, incorporating the newly acquired motifs of Renaissance design, added a novel and colourful feature to our parish churches.

One of the most poignant reminders of the hazardous politics of the reign of Henry VIII is to be found at Framlingham in Suffolk, in the splendid church that stands close to the castle of the Howards. Members of that family had been buried at Thetford Priory but at the Dissolution their tombs were moved to Framlingham where a new chancel was built for them and those that followed. The altar has now been moved farther west so we can move freely about in the great open spaces of this eastern extension and fully appreciate the monuments that so nobly represent the *dramatis personae* of some of the critical events of sixteenth-century England. The finest of them all is that of Thomas Howard, 3rd Duke of Norfolk (p 71), one of the grandest works of the Early Renaissance and particularly interesting because its rather French details are so much more advanced than the purely Gothic chancel that this duke built. Margaret Whinney in her *Sculpture in England, 1530-1830* offers evidence to suggest that this great difference in style is due to the fact that this monument was one of those removed from Thetford Priory and not completed until the 1560s, by the 4th Duke, when the tomb of his two wives was made, for the details of the effigies are identical in style.

Towards the end of the reign of Henry VIII there was a

struggle for power because the successor to the throne was but a boy, and the Howards and the Seymours were the chief contestants. The 3rd Duke of Norfolk was uncle to Queen Catherine Howard and an enemy of Wolsey, with aspirations to high office, but eventually the duke and his son Henry, Earl of Surrey, were accused of treason. The earl was executed but his father had a lucky escape when the death of the king saved him from the scaffold.

Henry Howard, called the Poet Earl of Surrey, seems to have been prone to rebellion for he had earlier been imprisoned for eating flesh in Lent and for breaking windows in London churches by shooting pebbles at them.[3] After his execution he was buried at All Hallows, Barking, by the Tower, but many years later his body was removed to Framlingham and an elaborate coloured monument erected, showing the earl and his wife Frances de Vere, daughter of the 15th Earl of Oxford, and their children kneeling about the base. There are two things that we must notice about this memorial. The countess wears her coronet but the earl's emblem of rank lies beside his head, on the cushion, in reference to his execution, and, what is more surprising, they are dressed in the fashions of 1614 when the monument was erected, in costume and armour that the earl would never have seen in his lifetime, for he had died at the Tower sixty-seven years earlier. However, we are able to see what the Poet Earl really looked like, for there are several versions of his fine portrait by William Scrots, and they hang in distinguished settings. One is at Parham Park in Sussex, in what must be the loveliest of all the great halls of Elizabethan England, another is at the end of the Cartoon Gallery at Knole, and others hang at Hampton Court and Arundel Castle, the seat of the present Duke of Norfolk. So at Framlingham we find a retrospective monument which, unlike that of Speaker Chute at The Vyne, makes no attempt to portray the costume of an earlier generation. There were good reasons for this. When the Poet Earl's younger son, Henry, commissioned this monument

76

in 1614 he was not only concerned with the commemoration of his father who had died so long before; he was also paying for the accurate portrayal of people then living and we can safely assume that this later generation would wish to be up to date, particularly the kneeling daughters who were married into the influential families of Neville, Berkeley and Scrope. Mrs Esdaile attributed this monument to the sculptor William Cure the younger, who had already completed his father's beautiful tomb of Mary Queen of Scots in Westminster Abbey.

Mention of Mary Queen of Scots is a reminder that there were further tragedies associated with the Howard tombs at Framlingham. The Poet Earl's elder son Thomas became the 4th Duke of Norfolk, and one might suppose that having a father who lost his head and a grandfather who missed the scaffold only by accident, the next generation would tread the labyrinth of Tudor politics with the greatest care. But no, the 4th Duke, who was considered the richest man in England and was a widower for the third time, was careless enough to attempt to further the Howard cause by a rash scheme to marry Mary Queen of Scots. This was during the reign of Queen Elizabeth, and he too was executed. His body was buried in the chapel of the Tower of London, but, unlike his father's, it was never brought back to Framlingham, so the great monument there has effigies of his two wives, Mary Fitzalan of Arundel and Margaret Audley of Saffron Walden, and there is a vacant space between them for the duke who never came back from London. But Thomas Howard, 4th Duke of Norfolk, does appear amongst his family at Framlingham, not on his own tomb but as the elder son kneeling at the base of his father's monument. This must be one of the few memorials in England of which it can be said that, long before the work was commissioned, father and son had both died on the scaffold.

The full significance of the figures of sons and daughters appearing on their parents' monument will be discussed in the following chapter, but while we are amongst the Howard tombs we must note some further points of interest. The figure of Mary Fitzalan of Arundel reminds us that it was through her that the Arundel branch of the Howard family was established. Her son Philip continued the family tradition by ending his life in the Tower when, as a Catholic, he had been accused of saying a mass for the success of the Spanish Armada. He was condemned to death but was allowed to linger on until he died there in 1595, and again we find the familiar story of burial in the chapel at the Tower and then re-burial later amongst the family tombs, but this time it was at Arundel instead of Framlingham. And so in the chancel of the church of St Nicholas at Arundel the Fitzalans are followed by Howards, and their tombs make a wonderful collection of monumental sculpture starting with the earls of Arundel and finishing with dukes of Norfolk, through five hundred years of history. In the Middle Ages the east end was collegiate and separate from the parochial part of the church, and it is still separate, being accessible only from the castle grounds, but through the original iron grille behind the parochial reredos there is a fascinating glimpse of the splendours that lie beyond.

There is a sequel to the story of the translation of the body of Philip Howard from the Tower to the church at Arundel, for he was eventually canonised and his body was again moved, this time only a few hundred yards to the vast Roman Catholic church of St Philip Neri. This great Victorian building, designed by Hansom, better known for his cab, crowns the romantic skyline of the town, its French Gothic outline complementing the turrets of the castle, and it contains this inscription: 'Remains of St. Philip Howard, Martyr and Earl of Arundel, 1557–1595, removed from Fitzalan Chapel, 1971.'

To return to the other figure on the Framlingham tomb, the missing duke's second wife was Margaret Audley whose father was Lord Chancellor Audley who succeeded Wolsey and was involved in Henry's marriages and the break with Rome. He was given Walden Abbey at the Dissolution, and on its site there rose the great house that bears his name, Audley End, which, after being rebuilt more than once, became for a while a royal palace for Charles II. The Lord Chancellor's monument is in the church at Saffron Walden but is on a much more modest scale than those at Framlingham.

Another statesman who became Lord Chancellor under Henry VIII, and who was involved in the suppression of the monasteries, was Sir Thomas Wriothesley. He too acquired one of the abbeys, in this case Titchfield between Southampton and Portsmouth, but he had a dozen other properties, mostly in Hampshire. It was Wriothesley who carried out the government orders that required the stripping of Winchester Cathedral in 1538 when, to avoid trouble, he wrecked St Swithin's shrine at three o'clock in the morning. At Titchfield the abbey church was destroyed but some of the buildings were converted into the mansion known as Place House, of which an impressive gateway remains. At the accession of Edward VI, when many noblemen were raised in rank, Sir Thomas became Earl of Southampton. In the struggle for power during the whole of that troubled period many titled heads were lost, including those of Seymour, Duke of Somerset, Dudley, Duke of Northumberland and the Howards that we have already noted, but Wriothesley died peacefully at his London house and was buried at St Andrew's, Holborn. As we have now come to expect amongst the Tudor nobility, his body was later removed and a gorgeous monument erected at Titchfield, retrospectively, some forty-four years after his death. It was not until the Lord Chancellor's son died in 1581 that we hear of a definite plan to erect two monuments and rebuild the south chapel at Titchfield, and A. L. Rowse in his *Shakespeare's Southampton* quotes from the 2nd Earl's will which required this to be done within five years of his death:

> . . . new side windows of stone to be made, the roof plastered, with pendants, being set full of my arms and all the walls plastered like

my house in Dogmersfield, and the same fair paved and divided
with iron grating from the church. Also two fair monuments there
to be made, the one for my lord my father (whose body I would
have thither to be brought and there buried) and my lady my mother;
the other for me, with portraitures of white alabaster or suchlike
upon the monuments.[4]

This is particularly interesting to us because eventually only one
monument was made, by Gerard Johnson, the Amsterdam
sculptor who settled in Southwark and whom we shall meet
again at Bottesford, and it was erected in the time of the 3rd
Earl. Perhaps he decided that the money left by his father didn't
run to two monuments so it was decided to make one very
large one (p 72). It is indeed a noble composition, in two tiers
with a great obelisk standing at each corner, and now that the
iron grating is no longer there we can examine it closely. On
the upper tier lies the figure of the Countess of Southampton
and on the lower level, to the south, her husband the Lord
Chancellor, the 1st Earl, and their son the 2nd Earl on the north
side. Lower still, kneeling round the base there are two daughters,
the 2nd Earl's wife and a son, the son who was the 3rd Earl of
Southampton by the time the monument was put up, and who
became Shakespeare's patron.

The young earl shown kneeling on the Titchfield monument
was a boy of eight when his father died, and he was put under
the guardianship of William Cecil, Lord Burghley, along with
two other young noblemen, the Earl of Bedford and the Earl of
Rutland. Eventually all three were involved in the conspiracy
led by the Earl of Essex towards the end of Elizabeth's reign.
Essex was executed, Bedford and Rutland escaped with imprisonment and heavy fines, and Southampton, although condemned
to die, was allowed to remain in the Tower until Elizabeth's
death. He and Rutland had been friends at Cambridge so it is
no surprise to find his portrait and that of his countess on either
side of the Stuart bed at Belvoir Castle, the Rutland seat.

Facing the great bed, with its flanking portraits, is the splendid painting of Henry VIII by a follower of Holbein, reminding us that the fortunes of the Wriothesley family were founded when Southampton's grandfather was active with Thomas Cromwell and the king in bringing about the suppression of the monasteries. It was Lord Chancellor Wriothesley who conducted the trial of Henry Howard, the Poet Earl of Surrey, so we have a link with those monuments at Framlingham.

The monuments of the earls of Rutland are in the church at Bottesford, near the point where Leicestershire, Nottinghamshire and Lincolnshire meet, in the Vale of Belvoir at the foot of the hill on which the castle stands. Some of these Rutland tombs will be considered in the next chapter but at this point we must mention another of the connections that link one monument with another, for it concerns the friendship of the young earls of Southampton and Rutland. We have already noted that the Wriothesley tomb at Titchfield was made by Gerard Johnson; this was when the 3rd Earl, who was to become Shakespeare's patron, was about twenty years of age. His friend Roger Manners, 5th Earl of Rutland, was three years younger and had at that time been involved in a very similar undertaking, for his uncle and father, the 3rd and 4th Earls, had died within a few months of each other and the Johnsons of Southwark had been employed to erect two great monuments at Bottesford in 1591 (p 72). Just as young Wriothesley kneels below the figure of his father at Titchfield in Hampshire, so young Roger Manners kneels at the foot of his parents' tomb at Bottesford in Leicestershire.

The guide book to Bottesford church is quite exceptional in that it deals fully with all the monuments in that unique collection, something that other churches with similar treasures might well copy, and it quotes from the Belvoir Castle accounts which give us a vivid picture of the setting up of these tombs. They were sent by sea from Southwark to the port of Boston and then the precious pieces of carved alabaster were loaded into fifteen carts, which needed a total of ninety horses to take them to Bottesford. It was a journey of about thirty-five miles, and we can picture that extraordinary cavalcade of carts slowly making its way along the fenland roads, such as they were, until they reached the limestone uplands. Then one of the carts broke down, and the accounts show payments for a night watchman to be on guard until an axle was mended, also for 'drinks for them that watched with him'. The walls of Bottesford church had to be cut away to accommodate these huge monuments and a Nottingham man was employed to paint the tombs and the wrought-iron grilles, the latter coming from Gainsborough by means of the Trent to Newark.[5] As at Titchfield, the grilles have now gone, but this does make it much easier to examine the details of costume and heraldry, and the inscriptions which are in English, adding greatly to one's enjoyment of these splendid monuments. It is interesting to note that Gerard Johnson and his son Nicholas rode up from Southwark to superintend the erection of these two works, and they had lodgings at the house of the local baker.

When Southampton died he was buried in the ancestral tomb at Titchfield, but Rutland was given a vast monument of his own, as large as those he had erected to his predecessors. This one was made by Nicholas Johnson, for it seems that Gerard had died by the time this further tomb was put up in 1616. This was the year of Shakespeare's death, and we find yet another connection, for the same Southwark workshop provided the well-known memorial in the chancel at Stratford-upon-Avon, but this time the work seems to have been done by Gerard Johnson the younger, a brother of Nicholas. The first two Rutland monuments were priced at £100 each, while the third tomb cost £150, but there were many extras involved in the earlier transaction of 1591; £12 for the shipmaster, £1 4s 6d for feeding the ninety horses, board and lodging for thirty-three workmen, as well as those drinks by the roadside when the cart collapsed. In all this we have to remember that in order to approach anything like the modern equivalent we have to multiply these amounts by at least twenty. There was an elaborate funeral when the 5th Earl of Rutland died, with the choir from Southwell Minster and a feast that required twenty-seven cooks;[6] if this seems rather a lot, we must remember that the Belvoir household amounted to over 200 people, even before counting the guests on such an occasion.

The tomb of Roger Manners, 5th Earl of Rutland, provides another example of the unexpected connections that we keep finding, for his wife who lies a little below him was the daughter of Sir Philip Sidney, and we saw her portrait at Penshurst. So the porcupine at her feet takes us back to our first chapter when we journeyed to Penshurst, Wilton, Ludlow, Cambridge and Westminster, and makes a link with countless houses and churches where the Sidney porcupine rears its gilded quills, or less fortunately as at Bottesford, where the quills have gone and only the holes for them remain.

Consideration of some of the later Bottesford tombs must wait until the following chapter, but enough has been said to indicate that this series of monuments is as rewarding as any in the parish churches of England, the more so because of the Belvoir accounts which add an element of social history, linking the church in the vale with the castle on the hill behind, where the story that starts with the monuments of earls is continued with the paintings and furniture of dukes.

Chapter 4

ROBED IN ALABASTER

I have just seen a collection of tombs like those you describe
. . . the house of Russell robed in alabaster and painted.
There are seven monuments in all; one is immense, in marble,
cherubim'd and seraphim'd, crusted with bas-reliefs and titles,
for the first Duke of Bedford and his Duchess. All these are
in a chapel of the church at Cheneys, the seat of the first
Earls.

Horace Walpole, in a letter to
George Montagu (1749)[1]

Since Horace Walpole's time there have been several more
monuments added to that remarkable collection at Chenies in
Buckinghamshire, making it one of the most splendid groups in
the whole country, comparable with those that we have already
seen at Edenham, Flitton, Croome and Bottesford. We recall
that Lady Anne Clifford's mother was a Russell from Chenies,
for the inscription on her tomb at Appleby mentioned this
early home of her ancestors, but when the Russells made
Woburn Abbey their principal seat they continued to use
Chenies as their burial-place, so the family portraits at Woburn
are more than twenty miles from their equivalent in monumental
sculpture. Like the tombs in the de Grey mausoleum at Flitton,
the Russell monuments can only be partially appreciated from
the church for they are in a private aisle, entry to which requires
special permission.

In an earlier chapter we noted a similar separation of the great
house from the family church in the case of Knole, in Kent,

where the principal Sackville memorials are at Withyham in Sussex, also on account of the location of an earlier family seat. For the same reason most of the monuments associated with the Cokes of Holkham Hall, in Norfolk, are fifteen miles away in the church at Tittleshall, but a much greater distance separates the house from the monuments of the Newdigates. Their family home at Arbury Hall, near Nuneaton in Warwickshire, is an eighteenth-century 'Gothick' building having elaborate decorations with plaster fan vaulting, but the Newdigates seen in portraits in that sumptuous setting have their sculptured memorials nearly eighty miles away at Harefield, near Uxbridge.

Fortunately for us such distances between a great house and its related monuments are rare, and we can in so many places enjoy seeing the house itself and then move off into the grounds to find a church on the estate where the memorials represent the people whose patronage of the arts produced the treasures that we have enjoyed. We can do this at Badminton and Kedleston, Belton and Lydiard Tregoze, Claydon and Knebworth, and a host of other places, but we must also be prepared to find instances of the church bearing a name different from that of the house with which it is associated. This is quite common and it can lead to difficulties. To determine the appropriate church you may have to refer to the county volume in Pevsner's *Buildings of England* or a *Shell Guide* or other county book. These connections that we are seeking are seldom mentioned in country-house literature or by the guides who are otherwise so helpful to visitors, so it is left to the individual enthusiast to make it a matter of personal discovery. Once you have located the appropriate church you can then begin to build up a sort of pictorial history of the art patronage of one family. It is a delight to go from long gallery or library to chancel or family chapel and meet, face to face, the very people who employed Kent or Gibbons, Adam or Gainsborough, Rysbrack or Capability Brown.

Including those great sets of monuments that we have already

85

mentioned we can compile quite a considerable list of churches that have a different name from that of the family seat to which the monuments relate. Not all the houses are open to the public, some are no longer lived in by the original family and in some instances there are monuments to be found in other churches too, but the more important displays of sculpture are indicated. This is a selection; a complete list would cover most of the counties of England.

Seat	Family	Church
Grimsthorpe (Lincs)	Bertie	Edenham
Knole (Kent)	Sackville	Withyham (Sussex)
Wrest (Beds)	de Grey	Flitton
Chillington (Staffs)	Giffard	Brewood
Belvoir (Leics)	Manners	Bottesford
Woburn (Beds)	Russell	Chenies (Bucks)
Arbury (Warks)	Newdigate	Harefield (Greater London)
Boughton (Northants)	Montagu	Weekley and Warkton
Ditchley (Oxon)	Lee	Spelsbury
Raby (Durham)	Neville and Vane	Staindrop
Althorp (Northants)	Spencer	Great Brington
Southill (Beds)	Whitbread	Cardington
Milton (near Peterborough)	Fitzwilliam	Marholm
Burghley (near Stamford)	Cecil	Stamford St Martin
Holkham (Norfolk)	Coke	Tittleshall
Tregothnan (Cornwall)	Boscawen	St Michael Penkevil
Haddon (Derbyshire)	Vernon and Manners	Tong and Bakewell

There were some families who owned estates in several parts of the country and have their monuments scattered far and wide, members of each branch of the family preferring to be buried in their local church rather than in the traditional resting-place chosen by earlier generations. This practice leads to a sort of genealogical tree that spreads its branches across the counties, so that we find Digbys at Sherborne, Dorset; Coleshill, Warwickshire; Stoke Dry and Tilton, Leicestershire; and doubtless in a dozen other places. Spencers and Throckmortons occur not only in the series of monuments at Great Brington and Coughton respectively, but in church after church throughout the Midlands and in London city churches too. We have already referred to the boast of the Seymours, that they could ride from Devon to London without leaving their own estates, and this we recall when we trace their houses, the sites of former houses, their monuments and their heraldry on inn signs all the way from Berry Pomeroy, near Totnes, to Maiden Bradley, Marlborough, Great Bedwyn and Salisbury Cathedral, and on to Westminster and their former London home at Somerset House. The Howards provide a similar sequence of houses and castles, portraits and monuments from Naworth, Greystoke and Corby in Cumbria to Castle Howard, Castle Rising, Audley End, Framlingham and Stoke-by-Nayland, and on to Westminster, Reigate and Arundel, and at all stages the work of the artist demonstrates the history of England, in visual terms, from Cumbria to Sussex.

Amongst the larger sets of monuments it is common to find a person appearing twice in the same church, first as a boy on the parental monument and then again on his own memorial, and in such cases it is always interesting to note the changes in costume and armour from one generation to the next, yet worn by the same person. In the case of daughters who marry into other families and go to live in another area the connections are stretched a little farther and the discoveries more unexpected. We can experience a wonderful sense of history when we find a young girl kneeling at her mother's side in the clothes of Shakespeare's day, and then come across that same individual in a church far away in another county as a squire's wife in the fashionable style of the time of Pepys. At Framlingham we have already found the kneeling son of the Poet Earl of Surrey achieving a special significance because his own figure is missing from the monument planned for himself and his first two wives.

But there is another kind of duplication which is not as easy to detect as those within successive family memorials in the same church. From time to time one comes across monuments in different parts of the country commemorating the same person, as an adult, and the reasons for this are various but always worth investigating. In the south transept of Hereford Cathedral there is a monument to Alexander Denton and his eighteen-year-old wife, with their little baby lying in the folds of its mother's mantle. Presumably the mother died in childbirth while at her parents' home at nearby Stretton Sugwas, but Denton belonged to Buckinghamshire and the family mansion there will be referred to in a later chapter. He married again and has a second memorial amongst the Denton family tombs at Hillesden, near Buckingham. This time the design has a local flavour, for it has much in common with those by Thomas Kirby at Chicheley and Turvey in the same district, characterised by strange sphinx-like figures around a sarcophagus, but no effigies.

Also in Buckinghamshire, but much more accessible than Hillesden, there is Gayhurst, on the A50 near Newport Pagnell. This church might be as little visited as Hillesden if it were not for a prominent sign on the main road. There is no village, and the perfect little Georgian church stands in the park, close to the handsome Elizabethan house. As well as the appeal of these two buildings, side by side in their lovely setting, a visit to Gayhurst is made more worth while because of the monument to Sir Nathan Wright and his son (p 89), aptly described by Pevsner as 'not only one of the grandest but also one of the most successful of its type in England'.[2] The Gayhurst monument is another instance of duplication, but with an unusual story. Sir Nathan Wright was the son of a Leicestershire rector to whom there

(*below*) Tong (Salop). Medieval and Renaissance monuments of the Vernon family who built much of Haddon Hall in Derbyshire

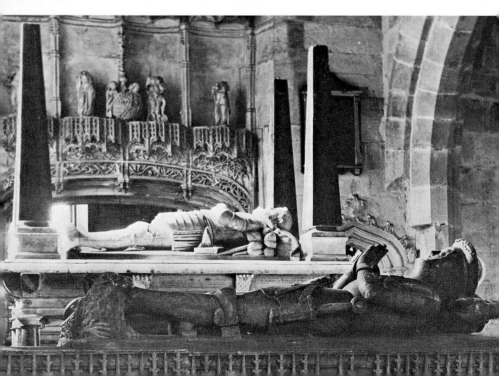

is a mural tablet in his church at Thurcaston, and the son ultimately owned several estates in that county, at Oadby, Belgrave and Barwell, and on the death of Sir William Villiers he purchased the Brooksby estate which had so long been in the hands of that famous family. It so happens that Sir William's monument at Brooksby, in the little church standing so prettily in the front garden of the hall, is another example of this same period.

Sir Nathan Wright married an Ashby from Quenby Hall, a fine Jacobean house not far from Brooksby, and he became Recorder of Leicester and Lord Keeper of the Great Seal under William III, delivering the seal into the hands of Queen Anne at her succession to the throne. He seems to have been involved in the political struggles surrounding Queen Anne and Sarah, Duchess of Marlborough, one account attributing his ultimate dismissal to the duchess, while another contemporary comment described him as 'of middle stature with a fat, broad face much marked by the small pox',[3] which makes his figure at Gayhurst, standing there with his son George, of special interest. Towards the end of his life Sir Nathan Wright's chief seat was at Caldecote, near Nuneaton, and it was his son who purchased the Gayhurst estate where, for some reason, he wished his father to be buried. There was a disagreement with the Gayhurst rector about this and Sir Nathan was honoured with only a modest tablet to his memory at Caldecote where it can be seen on the west wall of the church, which is yet another that stands in the grounds of the hall. Eventually his body was removed to Gayhurst when, by the terms of George Wright's will, the exquisite Georgian church was built in 1728, and the distinguished monument to father and son was erected in it. Perhaps there had been a change of rector or perhaps the early death of the son and the provision of such an admirable new church had put an end to the misunderstanding.

Another important personality of the William III and Queen Anne period has a notable monument with the same grandeur

F

and excellence as the Gayhurst one, and this too involves an interesting example of duplication. Sir Robert Clayton, Lord Mayor of London, stands with his wife under a vast baroque superstructure in the church at Bletchingley, Surrey, and at their feet is the pathetic figure of their little child in its baby clothes (p 89). Sacheverell Sitwell has called this monument 'one of the most entirely satisfying works of art in the whole kingdom',[4] and whether we agree with such superlatives or not, we cannot help but marvel at this great work by Richard Crutcher, an almost unknown sculptor. Sir Robert Clayton was a great benefactor of St Thomas's Hospital in London, and there is a statue of him by Grinling Gibbons in the hospital, but the unusual duplication connected with the Bletchingley monument concerns the figure of the baby, for this occurs again but in different clothes, and all alone, in the church at Ickenham where the child died forty years earlier.

Following the murder, in 1628, of George Villiers, Duke of Buckingham, the king's favourite who was born at Brooksby, a monument was made by the great Nicholas Stone and put up in St Thomas's church, Portsmouth, now the cathedral and not far from the scene of the murder. The unpopular Buckingham, therefore, achieved two memorials, for the better-known one is in Henry VII's Chapel at Westminster, already mentioned as making a link through his Manners wife with Bottesford church and Belvoir Castle, and through his daughter with that great painting of the Earl of Pembroke's family in the Double Cube Room at Wilton. Rare indeed are the instances of the same person commemorated twice as an adult in the same building, but this does occur at St Mary Redcliffe, Bristol, that wonderful church brought to completion by William Canynge, five times mayor and twice MP for the city. There is a large monument under an arched recess, showing Canynge and his wife, but close to it there is another one showing him in priest's vestments as Dean of the College of Westbury-on-Trym, for he took holy orders after the death of his wife.

William Cecil, Lord Burghley, and his son Robert, Earl of Salisbury, appear frequently in portraits, not only in their own great mansions of Burghley and Hatfield; they are familiar figures in countless other houses throughout the country. Their monuments, as one would expect, are in churches adjacent to their homes, namely St Martin's Stamford (p 90) and St Etheldreda, Hatfield, and both are impressive Renaissance works but quite different in character. To stand quietly and contemplate these huge tombs is to feel, in a very real sense, the history of England under the influence of these two statesmen in the reigns of Elizabeth I and James I. The two Cecils provide another example of duplication because, in addition to their tombs at Stamford and Hatfield, they both appear as subsidiary kneeling figures in Westminster Abbey on an enormous monument in St Nicholas's Chapel, commemorating Burghley's second wife. But this is not the end of the story; at the other end of the Abbey, under the north-west tower, they both appear again, this time with their wives in the form of miniature figures on Goscombe John's monument to their illustrious descendant the 3rd Marquess of Salisbury, three times prime minister to Queen Victoria. But there is an additional interest here, for the builder of Hatfield holds a plan of the house in one hand and a model of it in the other, a delightful example of the link between personalities and places. At Hatfield church there is a replica of the Goscombe John work, close to the monument of the 1st Earl, erected four hundred years earlier.

FATHER AND SON: MASTER AND SERVANT

Haddon Hall, standing on the hillside above the Derbyshire Wye, must be one of the best-loved country houses in all England. It is the perfect example of a fortified medieval manor house with little added in later years to upset the harmony of its outline of towers and battlements. It was the Vernons who built most of this fortress-house and the Manners who added the long gallery where the glittering mullioned windows look down on to the rose garden below. The beauty of Haddon's long gallery and the steps leading on to the terrace will always be associated with the popular but unreliable story of Dorothy Vernon's elopement with John Manners, and it was because of this marriage that the property passed into the hands of a junior branch of the family who held Belvoir Castle. Once again we can find the story told in terms of monumental sculpture, the relationship between house and monuments being such that we must consider it in some detail.

We start with the Vernon monuments, another of those grand groups that can be considered as having a place amongst the dozen best sets in England; but they are not anywhere near Haddon, indeed they are forty-five miles away at Tong, in Shropshire, where the family owned another property. Here the stately series of splendid tombs stretches right across the great collegiate church from the north transept to the south, and through to a special little chantry chapel founded by Sir Harry Vernon in 1515 (p 90). In this 'Golden Chapel', with a miniature fan vault with rich pendants and traces of gilding, there is another case of duplication in memorials, for Sir Harry's youngest son, Arthur, is commemorated by a brass as well as a delightful little figure high up on a bracket as if preaching from a stone pulpit. He was rector of Whitchurch and his unique little monument earns a special place in English art. Sir Harry Vernon did a lot of building at Haddon, as did his father and grandfather, each with tombs in the Tong series, but it is his eldest son Richard who concerns us most for he provides the link with the next part of the story. His monument at Tong has, at the end of the tomb-chest, a small figure of his son George who wielded such power at Haddon that he was called 'The King of the Peak' and he chose to be buried in his 'kingdom' at Bakewell, the nearest church to Haddon, so our story moves to Derbyshire.

Dorothy Vernon, the heroine of the legendary elopement with

94

John Manners, is shown as a daughter on the tomb of Sir George Vernon, 'King of the Peak', at Bakewell, and only a few feet away she kneels with her John on their own monument. Their eldest son George Manners is shown below, in a little niche, but at the opposite end of the aisle he appears again in his own right with his wife and children on a huge monument that fills the whole wall. Several of the children shown on this Manners memorial were born at Aylestone, just outside Leicester, and their names appear in the church register there. Evidence of the Manners ownership of the Aylestone estate is provided by their peacock crest on a painted panel in the church, tablets to Rutland household chaplains from Belvoir who were rectors here, a large sixteenth-century brass to the rector who married John Manners to Dorothy Vernon and, in this locality, Vernon Road, Belvoir Drive and the Rutland Arms. One of those children who kneel in the arched recesses on the Bakewell monument is of special significance for it was he, the second son, who eventually became the 8th Earl of Rutland and made Belvoir Castle his seat, following that branch of the Manners family that had long held the title.

So the story that started at Tong moves on from Haddon Hall and Bakewell church to Belvoir Castle and Bottesford church, and Dorothy Vernon's grandson who kneels on his parents' tomb at Bakewell gains a place for his own monument amongst that gorgeous series to the earls of Rutland which we have already noted in an earlier chapter. John Manners, 8th Earl of Rutland, was the last of a long line of earls to have monuments at Bottesford. His successor was made the 1st Duke in 1703, and by then the chancel was full to capacity. Later a mausoleum was built in the park at Belvoir, and from our point of view it is the portraits in the castle that take up the story. Amongst these portraits there is one by Closterman of the 9th Earl who became the 1st Duke, and another, by Kneller, of his duchess Catherine, daughter of Baptist Noel, 3rd Viscount Campden, of Exton.

Catherine Noel, of the Kneller portrait, also appears amongst the children shown on the lovely little relief panels beneath the figures of her parents on the huge Noel monument in the north transept at Exton, in Leicestershire, and to confirm our link with Belvoir Castle she is mentioned on the inscription as being 'now the wife of John Earl of Rutland', for this was before the dukedom was conferred. It is tempting at this point to embark upon the story of the Noels, their house and their monuments, but this must wait until the following chapter. What concerns us now is the relationship between two major works of sculpture, at Bottesford and Exton. Viscount Campden's monument at Exton is one of Grinling Gibbons's most impressive works, and it was erected in 1686 at a cost of £1,000 (p 107). At about the same time the Earl of Rutland was planning to commemorate his predecessors, and from the Belvoir accounts, fully discussed in David Green's life of Gibbons, it appears that, in the first instance, Cibber was approached but eventually the commission came to Gibbons and a design was produced that was in some ways similar to the Noel monument at Exton. It would be nice to know to what extent Rutland was influenced by the splendour of his father-in-law's memorial. It is not quite clear which came first, but the Bottesford work is a distinctly inferior version of Gibbons's design, so perhaps the execution of it was undertaken by another hand. The two churches are twenty miles apart, but it is instructive to compare these monuments and to relate them to the portraits at Belvoir and the kneeling figure on the tomb at Bakewell.

There are two other earls at Bottesford still to be mentioned. The largest of all that remarkable group of tombs is that of the 6th Earl of Rutland and it bears the well-known reference to witchcraft, a valuable contemporary record of the death of two sons and the trial for 'wicked practise and sorcerye' which took place in 1618–19. This monument also has a reference to the 'Spanish Match' when Buckingham and the future Charles I made the abortive journey to Madrid with a view to the marriage

of Charles to the Infanta of Spain. In this connection we note
that Katherine Manners who kneels at her parents' feet on this
tomb eventually married Buckingham, so she appears again on
his monument in Westminster Abbey. Another kneeling
daughter at Bottesford is to be found at Westminster, in St
Nicholas's Chapel; Elizabeth Manners on the 3rd Earl's tomb
married a grandson of Lord Burghley, and although her figure
is only a fragment of a former memorial, it does look across to
the great Cecil monument which we have already noted.
The 7th Earl of Rutland has a different monument from all the
others at Bottesford; it is a single standing figure provided by
Gibbons at the same time as that of the 8th Earl, and in the same
Roman fashion, but this is another example of a retrospective
memorial, put up forty years after his death.

Before we leave this story we must take a brief look at two
further family links which demonstrate the complex network
that develops when we study monuments. The wife of John,
8th Earl of Rutland, standing beside him like a Roman matron
on the Gibbons work at Bottesford, was a Montagu from
Boughton, near Kettering, and she is mentioned on the monument to her father in the church at Weekley, on the edge of
Boughton park; and the wife who stands beside Baptist Noel,
3rd Viscount Campden, on that similar Gibbons work at
Exton, was a Bertie of Grimsthorpe, daughter of that Earl of
Lindsey who accompanied the body of Charles I from Whitehall to Windsor, and whose monument we noted at Edenham.
So the sculptors, working under patrons who were closely linked
by family ties, bring us back to those monuments in Lincolnshire
where we began these journeys.

The Hon John Byng did not like Belvoir. He called it 'a
nasty stare-about castle', but we must remember that it was
the old plain mansion that he saw in 1789, looking as domestic
as the contemporary Nottingham Castle does today. In his
usual petulant manner he described it as a place 'where everything is in neglect and Ruin . . . Here is neither Grandeur of

Old Buildings, or of convenience of new'[5]. It was a few years later that the 'Gothick' towers were to rise upon the hill, looking north to the slender spire of Bottesford, the grander spire of Newark beyond, and further still to the towers of Lincoln. On this line of hills the far-off cathedral is the only rival to Belvoir and their towers seem to answer one another across twenty-five miles of level landscape. On days when the terrace at Belvoir is not available to the public you can enjoy a similar view by taking the nice open road to the ducal village of Woolsthorpe. This is not the village of that name that has Sir Isaac Newton's birthplace, but for those who wish to explore another aspect of the story of monuments and their relationship to the great house it is a place worth finding for the sake of the former churchyard. This is nowhere near the handsome nineteenth-century church in the village but high up in the woods, near where the lane to Harston is crossed by a bridge which carries the private drive from Belvoir Castle to the Grantham road. Here, in a clearing near the road, the site of the old church is marked by some heaps of stone buried in brambles. It is a strange, forgotten place, of interest only if you are prepared to grub about in the long grass and discover the inscriptions on the crooked headstones, for here lie some of the servants from Belvoir. There is a slate commemorating the 'first whipperin to his Grace the Duke of Rutland', one to a gardener at the castle and another to 'a native of Tilsit in Polish Prussia' who was a family servant for more than fifty years and was 'the deliverer under Providence of the famous Marquis of Granby when surrounded by the enemy'.

To discover the memorials to the household staff of a great estate is to add yet another dimension to our study, so it is always worth while searching amongst the tablets inside an 'estate church' as well as in the graveyard. At Turvey, in Bedfordshire, there are grand monuments to the Mordaunt family but on the outside wall of the chancel there is a brass inscription of 1612 which contains a delightful reference to the lords whose tombs are inside the church.

> Heare lyeth John Rychardson under this Wall
> A Faythfull True Servann to Turvey Old Hall
> Page to the first Lord Mordaunt of fame
> Servannt to Lewes Lord Henry and John
> Paynefull and Careful and Just to them all.

> Till Death Toke hys lyffe
> God Have Mercie of his Soule
> Amen.

Much has been written on the epitaphs to be found on church-yard headstones, usually concentrating on the more amusing verses, but a careful study of the 'servant situation' will reveal hitherto unsuspected details of this aspect of the great house. At Flitton there is a brass to Thomas Hill who was 'Receiver General to three worthy Earls of Kent, viz. Reginald, Henry and Charles'. His status enabled him to have a coat of arms and he wears an unusual cap with a decorative edge. Thomas Hill died in 1628, aged 101. At Spelsbury in Oxfordshire, another church from the list of those that have a different name from the house with which they are associated, there is a poignant inscription at the chancel steps to George Pickering who was for thirty years a servant to the Lees of Ditchley and was buried in 1645 as near to his beloved earls of Litchfield as his status would allow.

> Not to prophane (by a rude touch) the dust
> of his great masters, doe we bouldly thrust
> this aged servants bones: whose humble love
> an innocent ambition did move
> by creeping neere their tombes adored side
> to shew his body, not his duty, dy'de.

There are countless instances of stewards, gamekeepers, butlers and housekeepers, but for some of the nicest of such memorials we must return to Bakewell, where several employees of the 8th Earl of Rutland were buried. Presumably these were the people who administered the Haddon estate after the earl had inherited Belvoir and transferred most of the family resources to that other seat. Amongst them is a delightful brass of a Carolean servant named Latham Woodroffe with the most entertaining decorations worked into the inscription and surrounding margins, also a brass to a steward and to one of the earl's keepers whose son was a Bachelor of Arts and master of the Free School at Bakewell. Like Thomas Hill at Flitton, some of these employees had coats of arms in their own right.

Among memorials to servants who risked their lives in protecting their masters, and there are many of these, one of the most expressive is the beautifully lettered oval tablet in the church at Titchmarsh, Northants, commemorating Hugh Richard, a servant to Sir Gilbert Pickering.

. . . seeing a villain behind his master, ready to run him through, this brave young man, not having time to save Sir Gilbert any other way, threw himself between the swordspoint and his master, receiving the wound in his own body . . . The wound, tho' desperate, proved not mortal . . . He was after unhappily drowned as he was learning to swim in a pit in the river, since called by his name. Never was a servant more lamented.

MIDLAND CONNECTIONS

We have considered several of the grandest sets of monuments to be found in England, some in detail, such as Edenham, Tong, Bottesford, Croome and Framlingham, but others equally splendid have had to be mentioned only by name. Every area has its outstanding examples, ranging from the brilliant pageantry of Lydiard Tregoze, Great Brington, Chenies and Arundel to the individual works of distinction at Bletchingley (p 89), Redgrave, Withyham (p 35) and Langar, and then there are hundreds of places which just have rewarding monuments of one kind or another. A selection is given in Appendix 2, under counties. With all the major sets of monuments the interest lies not only in the costume and armour in a sequence of changing styles but also in the personalities involved, and the unexpected connections with other monuments in other churches. Let us take as an example a group of places in the Midlands that have related monuments which bring to life so many people who played their part in affairs of state as well as in local events.

Near to the point where Warwickshire, Northamptonshire and Leicestershire meet, a few miles from Rugby, a gracious William and Mary house stands in a park watered by the river Avon. It is the same Avon that runs to Warwick and Stratford, but here at Stanford Hall it is a modest stream not far from its source at Naseby. This is a peaceful place, for Rugby lies well beyond the Watling Street, the junction of two motorways is just out of sight, and the sound of the traffic scarcely reaches this tranquil spot. The railway line that once threaded its way along the valley had a little station here, with the attractive name of Yelvertoft and Stanford Park but its coming did not please Sarah, Baroness Braye, who 'reigned' at Stanford for so much of the nineteenth century. She thought it too close to the house, yet in her old age she seems to have made use of the railway, her carriage, horses and servants being put on the train. Like Lady Anne Clifford, two hundred years earlier, she kept diaries and a fascinating record of household expenditure, and these, quoted in Charles Lines's account of Stanford Hall, give us a vivid picture of the life of a great house.[6] Once again the monuments in the church and the portraits in the house complement one another.

Sarah, Baroness Braye, inherited Stanford from her forebears in the Cave family, and it was Roger Cave who built the present hall, the agreement with the architect and builder, William Smith of Warwick, being dated 1697. The old manor house was on the left bank of the Avon, near the church, but when the new site was chosen the situation arose in which the village and church remained in Northamptonshire but the hall and park were in Leicestershire, a complication for those who look up this place in county books. The church is one of those that must be visited by all who value our heritage of lovely things, for its monuments are exceptional in number and variety while the gorgeous windows of medieval glass make the whole interior a visual experience that is unforgettable. Then there is the woodwork, the delicately coloured seventeenth century organ case, and the display of Cave hatchments which, with the shields in the glass and on the monuments, make a brilliant pageant of heraldry that is unrivalled in our parish churches. The stone-paved floor space is open and uncluttered, and the monuments, instead of being closely confined in a Cave family chapel, are placed all around the church so that in the coloured light of green and gold, ruby and blue from jewelled windows this all forms a unique setting for enjoying five hundred years of English art.

We can start with the tomb of Thomas Cave which stands between two arches of the nave arcade. He died in 1558 but his recumbent effigy has early Tudor armour that is little different from that of the reigns of Henry VII and Henry VIII, but his wife has the up-to-date close-fitting cap that is seen in portraits of Mary Tudor, the young Elizabeth and Mary Queen of Scots. The marginal inscription, still in Gothic lettering, tells us that he was lord of the manors of 'Stanforde, Downe, Stormes-worth and Boresworth'. The last place is presumably Husbands Bosworth, which is quite near, but Downe and Stormesworth are particularly interesting because they are 'lost villages', long since depopulated and only to be found on the one-inch Ordnance Survey map if you know what to look for. Downton Hill is shown on the Northamptonshire side of the Avon, and Nichols in his *History of Leicestershire* describes it as 'anciently a village on the side of a hill, called to this day Down Hill or Down Town. Here have been turned up in ploughing, large foundation stones and causeys and in this hamlet was a chapel dependent on Stanford'.[7] Stormesworth is represented on the Survey map by the words 'Westrill and Starmor' spread vaguely across the area to the north of Stanford and adjoining Swinford, the next village. Here again Nichols helps by saying that the present Stanford Hall 'is in the lordship of Westrill or Wester-hill, with nine ploughlands in Stormworth' and he goes on to say that the north aisle of Swinford church was formerly known as the Stormer Aisle. For local historians who are investigating the sites of deserted villages this area is producing rewarding results.

At the foot of the Sir Thomas Cave tomb there are delightful panels showing rows and rows of kneeling sons and daughters, and these are of special importance to our story. Amongst the sons there is Roger, who inherited Stanford because of the death of his elder brother, so if you look for the second boy in the series you have a link with the Cecils, for Roger married Lord Burghley's sister Margaret. Amongst the daughters there is Margery, who married Francis Farnham who became Recorder of Leicester and MP for that city, and if you want to see Margery Cave again you must go to the church at Quorn, between Leicester and Loughborough, where she appears with her husband on an incised slab amongst the other memorials in the Farnham Chapel. For the next generation of Caves we must turn to the grandest of the monuments at Stanford, on the north side of the sanctuary where Roger's son Thomas lies beneath a canopied superstructure topped by the usual heraldry and strapwork (p 107). His wife was Eleanor St John, from Wiltshire, giving a link with that other marvellous series of tombs at Lydiard Tregoze, near Swindon, but the special feature of this monument is the miniature pavilion at one end, surmounted by an obelisk and containing a kneeling figure of the eldest son who was buried at sea after his death while a student at Padua. With its fresh colour and gilding this little masterpiece in alabaster is one of the delights of Stanford and our pleasure is the greater if we study it carefully and notice the clever way in which the designer has linked it with the adjoining row of brothers and sisters by means of a small lettered scroll which bridges the gap across to the main monument. The inscriptions here reveal not only the Padua incident but the unmistakable pride which Sir Thomas felt in being a nephew of the great Lord Burghley.

If we wish to follow up this connection we must go to the church of St Martin in Stamford, just on the edge of the park that surrounds Burghley House, and look there for a mention of the Caves. The Secretary of State to Queen Elizabeth lies within a sumptuous tomb on the north side of the sanctuary (p 90), and close by on the east wall of the Cecil chapel there is a wall monument to his parents. Three daughters kneel at the base and the inscription tells us that 'Margaret was first marryed to Roger Cave of Stanford Esq. of whom is discended Ser Thomas Cave'. We have already considered instances of people appearing first as a child on the parental monument and then again on their own, but we search in vain for Lord Burghley as a son on this memorial to his parents. The reason for this appears to be that, although his father died in 1552 and his mother lived on until 1587, their memorial seems to have been delayed until after the death of Lord Burghley himself, in 1598. So, presumably, with the costly monument to the great statesman being erected only a few feet away there was no need to show him as a son amongst his sisters; moreover, the inscription concerning his mother shows that Burghley was already dead by the time she was commemorated.

> . . . she lived to see her children and her children's children to ye fourth and fift generation . . . being a happy mother of ye most honorable Sir Wm. Cecill Knight of ye noble Order of ye Garter Lo. Burghley Lord High Trer of England who lyeth here by her.

If we were to trace all the Cave daughters of the several generations and find their husbands' monuments in churches far from Stanford we should need to cover many of the counties of England, and the familiar shield, in heraldic terms 'azure fretty argent', which occurs so many times at Stanford, would be a constant clue. But it will be sufficient if we demonstrate this genealogical exercise by reference to a few further places in the same area. We have already found Margery Cave, from that charming group of Stanford children, amongst the Farnhams at Quorn, but only a few miles away at Prestwold, in a church buried deep in the woods alongside Prestwold Hall, there is a great alabaster monument to Sir William Skipwith recording that his first wife was Margaret Cave of Stanford, another who could claim Lord Burghley as an uncle. It also tells us that they lived at Cotes, an adjoining manor to Prestwold, and here again this is a reference to a lost village. There is a present-day hamlet of Cotes, on the A60 near Loughborough, but the site of the old village can be traced by 'field marks' and there are fragments of the old manor house near to Cotes Bridge.

How often on these journeys we have found important monuments in a church that stands hidden in the park, close to the big house but remote from any village. This is so often the case that we need to acquire quite a technique, not only to find the obscure 'parish path' through thickets of rhododendrons but also to obtain the key before embarking on what could be half a mile of fruitless investigation. Some of the very best monuments are to be found in these circumstances, and one thinks of Croome and Gayhurst, Badminton and Exton, Wimpole and Claydon, Kedleston and Lydiard Tregoze, but Prestwold is one of the most securely concealed. A sign that points the way to the church, as at Gayhurst, Exton and Castle Ashby, usually means that the building will be unlocked, and when the house is open to the public then the adjoining church becomes one of the attractions and adds enormously to the understanding of the story of the family and its patronage of the arts. Stapleford, near Melton Mowbray, is one of these and is regularly open, but the church is accessible at any time by inquiry at the lodge;

even then you have to know where to find it, for find it we must if we are to follow up another of the Cave connections.

Stapleford church would be worth finding even if it contained no monuments. It is a little white 'Gothick' building like a pretty toy, decked out with pinnacles and shields of arms, and it stands all by itself in a clearing in the woods, perhaps the best of all settings for the quiet contemplation of visual history. The designer George Richardson exhibited his drawing of it at the Royal Academy in 1783, when it was Number 381 and entitled 'Elevation of a Church Building at Stapleford in Leicestershire, for the Earl of Harborough'. The furnishing is set lengthwise as in a college chapel, with little lights in rows along the seats, and the ribbed plaster ceiling is a reminder that Richardson was engaged in this branch of design at Kedleston Hall, and in his *Book of Ceilings* he is referred to as a 'draughtsman and designer to those eminent masters Messrs. Adam of the Adelphi'. There is a western gallery with a Sherard family pew, complete with fireplace, and in the nave a Sherard brass from the fifteenth century. It was a Sherard who married Abigail the daughter of Cecil Cave, yet another of the children of Roger and Margaret, with Lord Burghley as their uncle. Abigail's husband, Sir William Sherard, died in 1640 so the splendid white monument that she erected belongs to the reign of Charles I, which, after our visits to Croome and Elmley Castle, we have come to recognise as one of the best periods of English monumental sculpture. Lady Abigail seems to have been another of those interesting women who not only undertook important building projects, as seen in her extensions to Stapleford Hall, but who have also left us details of their households, for the guide book to the house contains a most entertaining inventory of her belongings. In the old kitchen there is a fine pair of portraits of Sir William and his Abigail, by Marc Gheeraerts the younger, and in the painting of the mother he has included her little boy who holds a bunch of cherries. Here we come to one of those nice relationships between portraits and monuments, linking the paintings

Page 107 (*left*) Exton (Leics). Baptist Noel, 3rd Viscount Campden, by Grinling Gibbons, 1686. An early example of the Roman manner which, later, was to supersede contemporary costume on monuments

(*right*) Stanford-on-Avon (Northants). Sir Thomas Cave, 1613. Attached to this monument to Lord Burghley's nephew there is a miniature memorial to a son who died at Padua

Page 108 (left) Lettice Knollys, Countess of Leicester. From the portrait at Longleat attributed to George Gower. She appears on monuments at Rotherfield Greys (Oxon) and Warwick

(below) Warwick, St Mary. The Beauchamp chapel. In the foreground the effigy of Richard Beauchamp, Earl of Warwick, d 1439. In the background the monument to Robert Dudley, Earl of Leicester, d 1588, and his third wife Lettice Knollys, d 1634

Page 109 (*above*) Low Ham (Som). The church, from the mounds and terraces of the lost mansion of the Stawells

(*right*) Swinbrook (Oxon). Fettiplace monuments. A few traces remain on the site of the manor house by the river Windrush

Page 110 (above) Hillesden (Bucks). The empty field at the end of the avenue where the house of the Dentons stood; (below) Chipping Campden (Glos). Garden pavilion remaining from the Hicks mansion

in the house with the sculpture in the little church in the park.

The child with the cherries in the Gheeraerts portrait in the old kitchen at Stapleford appears as one of the exquisite little figures on his parents' tomb, and again as one of the busts that form a sort of multiple monument to later generations, high on the wall above, similar to the busts at Edenham. His son became the 1st Earl of Harborough and has a grand monument on the opposite side of the church with figures in the Roman style by Rysbrack. As so often happens with these heroic Roman compositions, there is an opportunity of seeing what the earl really looked like if you look for his portrait in the house, for this shows him in the long periwig of the day. A similar contrast between the timeless classical monument and the fashionable contemporary portrait occurs in the case of the 5th Earl of Exeter who reclines with his Cavendish wife on an Etruscan-style sarcophagus in the Cecil chapel at St Martin's, Stamford, but appears in a full-bottomed wig at Burghley House.

But return to Stanford-on-Avon, there are further Cave monuments there which have connections that will lead us to Warwick and a collection of tombs even more famous than Horace Walpole's 'house of Russell robed in alabaster'. Behind the monument of Sir Thomas Cave, the one in the nave that first claimed our attention, there is a memorial to his brother Ambrose. There is no effigy, but in Stanford Hall there is a portrait of him, and he wears round his arm the garter in reference to the well-known story which tells of a ball attended by Queen Elizabeth. She dropped a garter, but when Sir Ambrose Cave picked it up she refused to take it, and he vowed that he would wear it for the rest of his life. Other portraits in the house show some of the personalities that we have met in connection with family monuments, including Lord Burghley, his son Robert Cecil the builder of Hatfield, and Lord Coventry whose monument we saw at Croome. In the ballroom there are some paintings with a strong Jacobite flavour, the portrait of the Old Pretender having a label which says 'James III, b. 1688 d. 1766.

This portrait belonged to his son Cardinal York, Henry IX'.
There is another of the Young Pretender, and in the near-by
corridor one of Cardinal York. It was after his death that Sarah,
Baroness Braye, purchased these Stuart portraits in Rome; also
from Italy is the marble pavement in front of Sarah's monument,
a grand Victorian Gothic piece at the west end of the church
(p 128).

Next to the simple memorial to Sir Ambrose Cave in the
north aisle of Stanford church there is a more elaborate monument to his daughter Margaret and her husband Henry Knollys.
His figure is recumbent but she lies stiffly on one side, head on
hand, a pose that suggests the gradual change to the taste of
later generations that preferred figures as in life. So instead of a
Cave daughter being found far away amongst the monuments of
her husband's family, here is an example of a daughter being
joined by her husband in her home church. Henry Knollys was
the son of Sir Francis Knollys whose wife, Catherine Carey,
was first cousin to Queen Elizabeth. Sir Francis was one of those
put in charge of Mary Queen of Scots during her captivity, and
he took part in her trial. He has a glorious monument at Rotherfield Greys, near Henley-on-Thames, and amongst his sons and
daughters shown on that tomb are Henry, whom we see at
Stanford, and the famous Lettice Knollys who was such an
interesting character in Elizabethan court circles (p 108). Lettice
was first married to Walter Devereux, Earl of Essex, but was
later associated with Robert Dudley, Earl of Leicester, when he
was still hopeful of marrying the queen. The subsequent marriage
of Leicester to Lettice Knollys infuriated Queen Elizabeth, for
she liked to have her Robin near her at court, but it is interesting
to note that when Leicester was no longer the queen's favourite
his place was taken by Robert Devereux, 2nd Earl of Essex, the
son of Lettice by her first marriage. This is referred to on the
inscription beside her monument at Warwick, so this is where
we must go to take up the next part of the story.

By a stroke of good fortune, when St Mary's church in

Warwick was destroyed in the great fire of 1694 the chancel and the adjoining Beauchamp Chapel were saved, and the lovely chapel that contains the tombs of Dudleys as well as Beauchamps remains as one of the greatest attractions of that famous town. The series of monuments starts with the alabaster figures of Thomas Beauchamp and his wife, 1369, lying hand-in-hand on an altar tomb in the centre of the chancel, and is continued with the brasses of Thomas Beauchamp II and his wife, now placed far too high up to be appreciated, on the south transept wall. Then with the next generation we come to the chapel itself, for this was built under the terms of the will of Richard Beauchamp whose monument, standing in the centre, is one of the most famous in the country. It is important not only because of its wonderful state of preservation but because its production is exactly documented in the contract made in 1449, so that we know the names of the carver, brass founder, goldsmith, marbler and coppersmith, also a Warden of the Barber Surgeons' Company, presumably called in to advise on the rendering of the head and the beautifully veined hands. Between the chapel and the chancel, half-way up the steps, there is a tiny chantry, an exquisite Gothic sanctuary in miniature, as if the chapel of Richard Beauchamp were not beautiful enough.

But we have come to Warwick to follow up the Knollys connection, so we must turn to the tombs of the Dudleys which, in this Gothic setting of the Beauchamp Chapel, make an instructive contrast between medieval and early Renaissance design. On the north side the huge monument to Robert Dudley, Earl of Leicester, and his third wife Lettice, rises to the full height of the chapel and has all the exuberance of its period (p 108). Leicester died in 1588, the year of the Armada, but Lettice, after marrying Sir Christopher Blount, lived until 1634 when, at the age of ninety-five, she died on Christmas Day. We are told that in her old age she retired to Drayton Bassett in Staffordshire where, at ninety-two, she could 'yet walk a mile in the morning',[8] and that she was benevolent to 'the grandchildren of her grandchildren',[9] reminiscent of the similar remark on the memorial to Burghley's mother. As well as the usual inscription on the tomb which recounts Leicester's offices of Master of Horse, Keeper of Forests, Parks and Chases, and his service in the Netherlands, there is a rare example of an additional inscription put up at the side of the tomb at the time of the death of Lettice. It is this that refers so delightfully to her 'capture' of the queen's favourite, the execution of her son Essex, her retirement to the country and her death on Christmas Day. This sort of human story, found on an inconspicuous wooden panel, brings history to life and makes the study of monuments so rewarding.

> She that in her youth had bene
> Darling to the Maiden Queene
> Till she was content to quitt
> Her favoure for her Favoritt
> Whose gould threed when she saw spunn
> And the death of her brave sonn
> Thought it safest to retyre
> From all care and vaine desire
> To a private countrie cell
> Where she spent her dayes soe well
>
> And sends His Angels from above
> That did to Heaven her Soule convay
> To solemnize His owne birth day.

We can relate the figures on this monument to the portrait of Lettice Knollys at Longleat, and those of Robert Dudley in so many places, including Penshurst where we have already seen him amongst his Sidney relatives. He was uncle to Sir Philip Sidney, to Ambrosia whose memorial we saw at Ludlow, and to Mary who became Countess of Pembroke and whose ruined house we found on the hilltop at Houghton in Bedfordshire.

Two other monuments in the Beauchamp Chapel at Warwick are of importance. First there is the pathetic little memorial
to the infant son of Robert Dudley and Lettice, on which the
inscription calls him 'the Noble Impe' and traces his ancestry
back to Richard Beauchamp whose splendid gilded figure is
only a few feet away. Ambrose Dudley, Earl of Warwick,
brother to Robert and uncle to the Imp, has a free-standing
tomb with freshly coloured heraldry and a single effigy. His
coronet is still upon his head and the inscription has a list of his
offices including that of 'pantler to the kings and queens of this
Realm at their coronations'. Members of a noble family were
usually buried in the church that had by tradition become the
resting-place of their ancestors, though we have already noted
some exceptions to this rule. Here at Warwick it is demonstrated
by the fact that Robert Dudley lies here, although his chief seat
was at Kenilworth Castle, and he died at Cornbury in Oxfordshire. His son 'the Imp' died at Wanstead in Essex, which was
another of Leicester's properties, and Ambrose died at Bedford
House, London, the town residence of his wife's family, the
Russells. Similarly, if we recall the monuments at Bottesford
for a moment, we can read there that the 3rd Earl of Rutland
died 'near Puddle Wharf in London', and the 7th Earl 'at his
house in the Savoy in the suburbs of London'; an interesting
comment on the size of the city in the seventeenth century.

Similar groups of churches could be chosen from other parts
of the country, but this journey to a group of places in the midland counties indicates how such a series of related monuments
provides first-hand evidence of personalities and events, so that
the people themselves emerge as characters in the story of
England.

Chapter 5

PASTURE WITHIN THE WALLS

John lord Stawel . . . pulled down a great part of the old
seat built by Sir Edward Hext, and began a most sumptuous
and expensive edifice, four hundred feet in length and one
hundred in breadth . . . The whole he did not live to see
complete, although it cost him upwards of one hundred
thousand pounds, to raise which sum most of the estate . . .
was sold by his trustees, who thought proper to let this
monstrous fabrick run to ruin . . .

Rev John Collinson,
The History of Somersetshire (1791)

Collinson's account of the mansion of the Stawells at Low Ham,
in the centre of Somerset, was written a hundred years after the
house was abandoned, and today its site is marked by a series of
mounds and terraces with a high stone wall, which, although
broken down in places, lends an air of grandeur to the place.
Even if one knew nothing of the history of Low Ham the sight
of these long white limestone walls enclosing an area of pasture
on the hillside near the Langport road would lead one to suspect
the existence of a former mansion. Although never completed,
the sum of £100,000 seems to have provided plenty of splendour, for Collinson mentions that 'three state rooms at the
south end were finished in the most elegant stile; the ceilings
decorated with very superb paintings'.

As so often happens, the church remains as a poignant
reminder of the vanished house of Low Ham, Indeed, it dates
from the time of the earlier house of the Hext family. This
beautiful little church seems to have been begun in the early

1620s and then completed in 1669 when the Civil War and Commonwealth were safely over, so it not only survived the hazards of those troubled years but also the pulling down of the Hext mansion and the ultimate destruction of the 'monstrous fabrick' that was built alongside. Now it remains, stranded for ever in the middle of a field, the tide of events having swept away the adjoining house (p 109). There is no churchyard, no protecting wall and no path to the door; it stands quite literally in a field, the grass kept down by the cattle from the neighbouring farm that graze about its walls, while higher up on the terraced slope the fowls scratch about where once stood the state rooms with painted ceilings.

After the first impression of something left behind by mistake when the family moved away, it is a surprise to find the church at Low Ham so beautifully kept. It was a chapelry of the mother church at High Ham, a 'gentleman's chapel' built for the convenience of the family and all its staff, and as such it could so easily have been swept away with the rest of the manorial buildings, but fortunately for us it remains as a rare and lovely example of the Gothic Survival of the early seventeenth century. In such a church, on the site of a great house, one immediately hopes for monuments that will tell the story of the family and interpret the puzzling fragments on the hillside, and here we are not disappointed. Sir Edward Hext who began the church, but died in February 1623/4, has a tomb in the north aisle with recumbent effigies of himself and his wife Dionysia. It was their daughter Elizabeth who married Sir John Stawell of Cothelstone and brought Low Ham into the Stawell family, so it is to Cothelstone that we must go in order to follow the next part of the story.

At the southern end of the Quantock Hills, overlooking Taunton, there is a prominent clump of beeches, visible from all over the county, and near by are the scanty remains of Cothelstone Beacon. Below, on the west side of the hill, lies Cothelstone itself; there is no village, and the passing motorist could miss the place entirely, but one should stop and look through the archway that leads to the manor house. Beyond lies a further gateway and then the house itself, an attractive irregular building in pink stone, and if you look carefully you will see the pinnacles of the church tower just showing above the house, like an extra bunch of chimney stacks. Access to the church presents quite a problem unless you are lucky enough to notice a little faded board hidden in the grass by the first archway, saying 'This way to church'. So you feel encouraged to walk boldly up the drive, turning aside at the second gateway to find a little path between farm buildings, past a row of cottages with a medieval doorway, and on round the back of the house until you discover the church.

Cothelstone church is worth finding, for it contains Stawell monuments that amplify the story of the lost mansion at Low Ham. Much the earliest is a pair of figures of a knight and his lady, from about 1400, probably Sir Matthew Stawell and his wife, Eleanor Merton. This monument repays very careful study for the details are exquisite, from the angels at the woman's head to the squirrels at her feet, her intricate headdress and buttoned sleeves, and the rare additional pieces for eye protection on the man's head armour. Then from quite a different age, but equally fine in detail, are the alabaster figures of Sir John Stawell and his wife from the early seventeenth century, and after that we must turn to a wall monument on the south side of the chancel, less spectacular but very informative. Like those discussed in an earlier chapter it refers to troubles endured during the Civil War, and it commemorates the John Stawell who married Elizabeth Hext, thus acquiring Low Ham, to which he retired after the destruction of Cothelstone. Collinson puts it in these words:

Being a person zealously affected to the cause of his Sovereign Charles I, for whom he raised at his own expence three regiments of horse, one of dragoons, and another of foot, he exposed himself to the malevolence and persecution of the parliament, who imprisoned him in Newgate, sold his lands, cut down his woods, and demolished his house at Cothelstone, which had been the residence of his family for many generations. He lived, however, to see the Restoration, and retiring to his seat at Nether Ham near Somerton, there died Feb. 21, 1661–2, and was conveyed with great funeral pomp to Cothelstone, and interred in that parish church.[1]

When Cothelstone was so badly damaged that the Stawells decided to make their home at Low Ham, the church there was still unfinished, a fact that may have influenced the family in thinking it more appropriate to undertake the solemn ten-mile journey when the Royalist's body was 'conveyed with great funeral pomp to Cothelstone'. His son Ralph completed the church at Low Ham and his monument stands in the south aisle; there is no effigy but a splendid mural design with a relief of military symbols, and, like the Hext tomb on the opposite side of the church, it has its original iron railings. The inscription tells of his father's loyalty to Charles I, and there is an additional panel at the base which commemorates Ralph's son, yet another John, who began to rebuild the house in the grandiose manner described in Collinson's account. Perhaps he wanted to follow the example of his wife's family, for he married Margaret Cecil, daughter of the Earl of Salisbury, who must have been familiar with Hatfield and Burghley.

Standing on the hill above Low Ham church, amongst the mounds and terraces, looking across the plain to Glastonbury and the far line of the Mendips, it is nice to recall that the one-inch Ordnance Survey map names this viewpoint Hext Hill, and that another vanished house, far older than the mansions of the Hexts or the Stawells, was unearthed in the fields below. During World War II a Roman villa was discovered here, and subsequent excavations revealed baths with several rooms, a furnace and hypocaust, and a splendid mosaic showing the story of Dido and Aeneas. So, 1,500 years before John Lord Stawell planned his house, others had chosen this green cup in the hills for their own 'sumptuous and expensive edifice'. There is another point to remember about Low Ham: a little of the Stawell mansion can still be seen, for a gateway was removed and re-erected at Sparkford where it stands at the entrance to Hazlegrove House, now the Junior department of King's School, Bruton, at the junction of the Ilchester and Yeovil roads.

At Swinbrook, near Burford in the Cotswolds, there is even less by which to remember the lost manor house, for no impressive walls surround the site, and the traces of terraces and fishponds can be seen only by taking the footpath across the fields on the way to the lovely little church of Widford. But the family that owned the manor is splendidly remembered by the monuments in Swinbrook church, in a series so striking that one wishes that the great house still stood above the winding waters of the Windrush. Here, more clearly than anywhere else, can be seen that strange manner of showing figures reclining with head on hand, resting stiffly on one elbow (p 109). To accommodate six members of the Fettiplace family on one side of the tiny chancel they are stacked up, one above the other, on shelves within two huge architectural surrounds. They look as if they had been suddenly roused from an uncomfortable night in bunks, and you cannot help feeling that as soon as you close the church door they will all thankfully shift their position and change over to the other elbow. The difference between the two groups is worth studying, for one is Elizabethan in feeling, with obelisks and strapwork and an almost medieval angel at the top, and the figures wear the armour so often seen in that period, whereas the other group, nearer the altar, shows a rather more mature classicism and two of the figures have the wigs and cravats of a later age. The later figures are still wearing armour but it is of the Carolean type, representing what is almost its last appearance in monuments. Then, as a third stage in this development of taste and fashion, outlined in Appendix 1, you can turn to the opposite wall and enjoy the sophistication and technical mastery of the beautiful monument to Sir George

Fettiplace, a little masterpiece of 1743 by James Annis. There are also good brasses on the floor beneath, so this little chancel at Swinbrook is rich indeed and brings to life, with a mixture of quaint and elegant artistry, the people whose house once stood here.

The site of a demolished mansion is sometimes marked by considerable architectural remains, recalling more clearly than Low Ham or Swinbrook the splendour that has been swept away. Perhaps there is a handsome gate pier such as we saw at Spilsby at the beginning of these journeys, or a series of them standing in majestic pairs around an empty field, as you can see at Hamstead Marshall near Newbury, looking like a stage-set for a drama that is finished, when all the characters have long since made their exits. A little farther north the noble gate piers remain from Coleshill House, so tragically burnt down in 1952, and nearer to Abingdon there is a similar story to be told at Besselsleigh, with all the familiar ingredients of a church in the park, with hatchments and tablets of the Lenthalls, but all that remains of the family mansion, at one time owned by the Fettiplaces, is one elegant gate pier close to the church.

Stables are usually allowed to remain long after the house has gone, for they can easily be converted into a convenient-sized residence for a later generation, or used for farm buildings, and in every county there are places where the church and the stable block stand together in a park, with an empty space beside them, a space that speaks of a changed social and economic pattern. One thinks of Clumber in Nottinghamshire; Stoke Edith near Hereford; Draycot Cerne, Wilts; Wheatfield, Oxfordshire; and Blatherwyck, Northants; but where else is the empty space more eloquent of departed grandeur than at Claverton, near Bath? Here there are the gate piers and the converted outbuildings, the church and the noble trees, but behind the gates there rises a series of terraces like a grand stairway ascending step by step to . . . nothing. The house that replaced the old manor was built high on the hill above the Avon valley and now contains the American Museum; the new setting gives the most wonderful prospect, but how glad we must feel that such dramatic evidence of the earlier manor was allowed to remain.

At Claverton there is a coloured monument to the Bassetts who were here in the heyday of the old manor house. Draycot Cerne has tablets to the Longs, and near them are photographs of the adjoining house which was standing until 1920. At Stoke Edith the monument to Paul Foley reminds us that it was his house that was being built when Celia Fiennes rode this way on one of her journeys in 1698. In her diary she tells of

> Mr. Folies new house which was building and will be very fine when compleated . . . with rows of trees to the river; the roof is covered with slatt which shines . . . its adorn'd round the edges with stone figures and flower potts; there is a noble Parck and woods behind; it will be very fine when finished, now I saw it only in the outside shell and platform.[2]

In 1955 it was once again only an outside shell and platform, there were demolition contractors' huts in the grounds and the shining slates were being stripped. Now only the converted outbuildings remain, and there is a space on the hill, but the lodges are still there, the one on the Hereford side having a delightful *trompe l'oeil* window, and there is always Mr Foley's classical church to see, with its odd truncated spire rising above the trees. In all such places where the church remains we must look for monuments in order to recapture the great days of the house. Here in alabaster and marble is the visible evidence of those who were the patrons of the carvers and the plasterers, the portrait painters, architects and gardeners, and those who sat on the now-faded crimson cushions in the squire's pew. Even though the house has gone, and their servants and carriages have departed, their heraldry still glows from tombs and hatchments; they lie there in their ruffs and farthingales and their children kneel in orderly rows, wearing pretty caps and collars. You can almost hear their laughter in the garden that has now become a forsaken field.

THE FORSAKEN FIELD

To find Hillesden, which is hidden away in deep country near Buckingham, you need a good map, for the devious lanes running through open fields without hedges lead nowhere but this remote village. But nobody could call it a 'dead end'; the church is such a joyous thing and the field beside it is steeped in history. So when you have enjoyed the elegant chancel with its rare cornice of angels, the Denton monuments and the family pew, the lovely glass and the upper chamber with a peep-hole down into the chancel, then you must go out into the field adjoining the churchyard on the eastern side and look around at the clues that tell of a vanished house (p 110). Along one side there is a wall with traces of openings and then, leading from this grassy space, an avenue of noble trees goes marching across country towards Claydon. Hillesden has not always been a peaceful place; during the Civil War there was fighting, destruction and heartbreak here, when the house of the Dentons stood beside this lovely church. In those days it must have been even more remote, but the bitter struggle between King and Parliament did not pass it by; Claydon was not far away and the Verneys were very much involved, for Sir Edmund Verney had married Margaret Denton of Hillesden.

From the family letters quoted in *The Verneys of Claydon*, edited by Sir Harry Verney, we get a vivid account of the anguish that must have been felt in that household when Sir Edmund decided that he must support the King even though his son Ralph had taken the oath of allegiance to Parliament. In the end, the father lost his life at Edgehill and the son went into exile, while Dr Denton of Hillesden, who was Ralph Verney's uncle, did much to keep the two families together through all their adversities. For the preservation of Claydon House a 'protection' was granted by the King, and another by Parliament, but no such immunity was obtained for Hillesden, and in 1644 it was besieged and set on fire. Sir Alexander Denton was imprisoned in the Tower, and from there he wrote to his steward to ask him if the damage was irreparable.

> . . . take a view of the house that was burnt upon Tuesday, that I may have certain information of what destruction is fallen upon me, and whether it be possible to rebuild those walls that are standing, if the distractions of the times should settle.[3]

Another house was built on the site before the 'distraction of the times' had settled, for a letter of 1648 quoted in the Buckinghamshire volume of the *Victoria County History* says that 'they are building there again and intend to set up a little house where the old one stood'. This must have been the house seen by Celia Fiennes when she came to Hillesden, in about 1694, to see 'a house of Mr. Dentons . . . which stands in the middle of a fine Parke; the house stands on a riseing in the middle and lookes very well'.[4] Later Dentons were related to the Cokes of Holkham and it was the famous agriculturalist, 'Coke of Norfolk', later Earl of Leicester, who eventually disposed of the Hillesden estate, sold the elaborate fittings of the family pew and demolished the house, early in the nineteenth century.[5]

As one would expect, the churches of Hillesden and Middle Claydon both have monuments that illustrate the story of the Dentons and Verneys; in the one they recall the empty field and the avenue of trees, but in the other the house is still very much part of the scene, though rebuilt at various times during the eighteenth century, with splendid interior decorations. The Denton monuments are a little difficult to follow because each generation seems to have produced an Alexander, including the one whose memorial we saw repeated in Hereford Cathedral. Dr William Denton, of the Civil War period, was physician to both Charles I and Charles II, and his memorial tablet bears a tribute to his happy disposition, a quality which must have been a great blessing when Hillesden was a scene of fire and bloodshed. Another Alexander has a fine eighteenth-century monument signed by Henry Cheere whose work we noted at Edenham.

The church at Middle Claydon is, for its situation, perhaps the most memorable of all those that stand in the grounds of a great house, for it is prettily perched on top of a mound in the garden. Amongst several good monuments there is a large one erected by Ralph Verney, when he returned from exile, to commemorate his parents and others of his family. This is another of those multiple memorials of which we have already seen several examples, and it is by Edward Marshall whose workmanship we saw in the fireplaces and portico added by Chaloner Chute to The Vyne. Documents exist which show that there were to have been two ambitious monuments but eventually, as happened at Titchfield, only one combined work was commissioned. Here is another instance of the sorrowful story that often lies behind such monuments. Sir Edward Verney was reluctant to take sides in the Civil War, and he wrote 'I do not like the quarrel, and do heartily wish that the King would yield and consent to what they desire.'[6] He felt certain that he would lose his life in defending policies which went against his conscience, and in the end he died holding the Royal Standard so firmly that his hand was grasping it although his body was never found. His ring was still intact, containing a miniature of the King, and this is still at Claydon House, but the hand holding a piece of the standard was buried beneath his monument in the little church in the garden. The bust of his wife, Margaret Denton, recalls the loss of the house at neighbouring Hillesden, and there is an unexpected link with Stanford-on-Avon through one of the Caves marrying a Verney of Claydon, which accounts for the portrait of Sir Edmund, the Standard Bearer, hanging in the green drawing-room of that Leicestershire house.

The search for deserted houses reveals a surprising variety of sites, from the empty field with a length of wall to the substantial ruin looked after by the Department of the Environment, and between these two extremes there are countless places that repay a careful study on the ground, with some work on county histories and a large-scale map. Even if we confine ourselves to those lost houses for which there is evidence in the church and its monuments we shall find that the exploration takes us to a remarkable diversity of sites. The village of Sapperton stands high above a wooded Cotswold combe and the church occupies a wonderful position on a slope with a view down to the Golden Valley, a prospect that was shared by Sapperton House when it stood just below the church on the north side. Its site is clearly marked by a grassy terrace and we can reconstruct the whole of the idyllic scene with the help of Kip's engraving which hangs in the church. There is special interest here because bits of the house can still be seen, for they were built into a romantic piece of make-believe called Alfred's Hall, hidden deep amongst the glades of Cirencester Park. This was done when Lord Bathurst incorporated the Sapperton estate into his vast landscape schemes in the eighteenth century and destroyed the old manor house of the Atkyns. The family had another property at Pinbury Park, a mile or two to the north, and here lived Sir Robert Atkyns, the author of *The Ancient and Present State of Gloucestershire*, who has a monument in Sapperton church by Edward Stanton, son of the Stanton whose work we have seen at Penshurst and Elmley Castle. The Gloucestershire county historian reclines in the relaxed manner of the Queen Anne period, with a long wig and, appropriately, he holds a book in his hand. There are other important monuments at Sapperton including one of very high quality to Sir Henry Poole, 1616, with a series of kneeling figures and all the familiar ornamental devices of the Jacobean age. This enjoyable church also contains woodwork from the destroyed house, adding to the delightfully

Page 127 (above) Chipping Campden (Glos). Sir Edward Noel and his wife Juliana, heiress of Baptist Hicks. Erected by Joshua Marshall in 1664; (below) Exton (Leics). Detail from the monument by Grinling Gibbons showing children of the 3rd Viscount Campden, see p 107

Page 128 (above) Bramfield (Suffolk). Elizabeth Coke, d 1627, by Nicholas Stone. Detail from a monument of the great period of the reign of Charles I; (below) Stanford-on-Avon (Northants). Baroness Braye, d 1862, by Thornycroft. The Victorian enthusiasm for the revival of Gothic forms

domestic atmosphere which it acquired when much of it was rebuilt by the Atkyns in Queen Anne's day.

Although a grass-grown terrace and solitary gate piers can be so eloquent, a pile of ruins will add an extra touch of the picturesque; they have an air of romance like an early nineteenth-century water-colour. If a church stands alongside the broken walls of the house, the feeling of anticipation is intense as we push open the ancient door and eagerly look for monuments. At Moreton Corbet in Shropshire you enter the cool church and stand amazed at the richness of the armour and costume, and the freshly coloured heraldry with shields held from above by ravens and muzzled bears and supported from below by white owls and golden elephants. It is a herald's delight, and it all has so much more meaning because you can then look out from the church windows to the gaunt silhouette of ogee gables and empty casements of the house of the Corbets. It is a very grand ruin of a house added to a much earlier castle, and the distinguished Renaissance details and the general air of careful restoration are all reminiscent of Kirby Hall in Northamptonshire. But Kirby has no church, and Moreton Corbet has the advantage of being able to show us the people, so that we can pass from the contemplation of noble windows and fireplaces to the Corbets themselves, their heads upheld by ravens or 'corbies', while their dogs worry the hems of their scarlet gowns.

Hampton Gay, in Oxfordshire, presents a very different picture. First of all you have to find your way, for there is no proper road and even when you have located it on the map, the means of access is not very clear. Go to Shipton-on-Cherwell, near Woodstock, and then find the footpath that takes you over the humpbacked bridge of the Oxford canal and follow it across the meadows to the river Cherwell; then across more meadows until you reach the railway which is crossed by one of those 'sleeper walks' that allow you to pick your way over the tracks. In the days of steam there was an extra pair of rails in addition to the main Oxford–Banbury line, and a little toy

H   129

train of the 'push and pull' variety used to run to and fro from Woodstock, a pretty thing which did nothing to disturb the tranquillity of these water-meadows. The isolated church of Hampton Gay stands in a field by the railway and if, having got this far, you find it locked, which is not at all surprising, and if you have failed to find the key before setting out from Shipton, then you will have to content yourself with pressing your nose against the windows to catch glimpses of the modest monuments and tablets that adorn the walls. At least they will assure you that people once lived here, so you can then persevere across another field and rummage about in a spinney until you find the burnt-out fragments of their mansion, remote and forgotten.

At Wadham College, in Oxford, the central feature of the principal façade in the main quadrangle is one of those exercises in the classical orders which are so typical of the early Renaissance era of college development, and amongst its pilasters and entablatures there are three figures, James I, and Nicholas and Dorothy Wadham. The foundation of the college was put in hand by Nicholas before his death in 1609 but it was left to his widow to carry out his wishes, the buildings being completed in 1613. Dorothy died five years later and a monument was erected to their memory in the north transept of Ilminster church, in Somerset. Only a few yards away there is a large brass to a fifteenth-century Wadham knight and his mother, with an elaborate system of canopies, on a tomb chest with excellent detail, so together these Wadham memorials, both with important brasses, make an instructive contrast in costume and armour, inscriptions and architectural accessories, in the Gothic and early Renaissance traditions. It is interesting to note that because the monument to Nicholas and Dorothy Wadham is so awkwardly placed in the corner of the transept the inscription at the foot of the brasses is set upside down so that it can be read, yet it was thought necessary for the figures to be in the traditional eastward-facing position (p 131). There are further inscriptions

Ilminster (Som). Brasses of Nicholas and Dorothy Wadham, founders of Wadham College, Oxford; d 1609 and 1618. A moat marks the site of their house at Merefield

against the wall above the tomb, as part of the architectural background, and these contain an interesting reference to the founding of the college:

> He still shines with a great light that glitters in the east. Do you not see? Look at the towers set on the other side of Isis where he built habitations for the Muses and lofty temples to God. There you behold the rays of Wadham's countenance.

The founders of Wadham College lived at a house called Merefield, near Ilminster, and this fact is mentioned not only on the Ilminster brass but also on a very similar one at St Decuman's church, above Watchet on the Somerset coast, for Nicholas Wadham's sister, Florence, married Sir John Wyndham, and the male figures on the two brasses are almost identical. The same engraver was probably responsible for similar brasses of the Wyndham family at Felbrigg in Norfolk. It has been suggested that Wadham College was built by Somerset masons, for there is a touch of the rural vernacular about its unassuming proportions; in any case it would be nice to have Merefield for a comparison, but alas, only a ghost of the house remains. It has been variously spelt Merifield, Merrifield, and, on the half-inch map, Merryfield, but on the one-inch Ordnance sheet it is marked 'Moat', and this is all you will find if you set out from Ilminster in search of the spot where the idea of the Oxford college first took shape.

At the village of Ilton, a few miles north of Ilminster, the church contains a tiny brass of a child in swaddling clothes, and the inscription bids us 'Pray for the soule of Nycholas Wadh'm sone to Sir Nycholas Wadh'm, Knyght and Capten of the Ile of Wyght'. This is a different Nicholas, but the Captain of the Isle of Wight was the grandfather of the founder of the college.[7] Along a narrow lane to the west of Ilton church there is a pretty row of almshouses, founded by our Nicholas in 1606, so we seem to be on the right track in our search for Merefield. The lane continues, and crosses the remains of the old canal that used

to run from Taunton to Ilminster. The canal's successor in the
the transport age, the railway line from Taunton to Ilminster,
which killed the canal, is now dead too, its deserted cutting
still crossed by a bridge. So there are other ghosts here besides
those that haunt the abandoned site of Merefield. The lane that
we have been following becomes no more than a field track
at a point where a cottage stands, and the name on the gate,
'Merryfield Cottage', is our cue for taking to the fields and
making straight for some trees in the distance. In good weather
this must be a pleasant spot, in spite of a derelict airfield not far
away, but on a winter day with the Blackdown Hills obscured
by driving rain it is all very eerie. After tramping through a
few hundred yards of wet grass, that clump of trees proves to
be the end of our journey, and we stand on the edge of a moat,
with a causeway leading to the central island. The water looks
inky black and the trees that bend over it have draperies of
grey lichen, like sinister shrouds, and there are no birds. A few
fragments of stone litter the island site of the home of the
Wadhams, once bustling with the life of an active household,
and as we stand there, surrounded by the dark water, we can
but try and picture them as they appear on their brasses at
Ilminster, in stained glass at Brockley, near Bristol, and at their
own college in Oxford, in stone in the quadrangle and in
portraits in the Great Hall and the Master's Lodge. Merryfield
is a pretty name, and it must have been appropriate, for Thomas
Fuller described the house as 'an Inn at all times, a Court at
Christmas'.[8] Today, even at Christmas, that moat strikes chill
and the bare trees shelter nothing but scattered stones.

All three sisters of Nicholas Wadham have monuments in
the West Country, helping us to picture the personalities of
Merefield. We have already noted the one who married Sir John
Wyndham of Watchet, but there is another at Puddletown in
Dorset, on the brass of her husband Nicholas Martyn,[9] of the
family that owned the lovely house of Athelhampton, and a
third is on a monument of coloured alabaster, by Baldwin of

Stroud, in the nave of Bristol Cathedral. She was first married to a Strangways of Melbury House in Dorset and then to Sir John Young who built the great house that stood on the site now occupied by the Colston Hall, in Bristol; another instance of a vanished mansion represented by a monument, but the Red Lodge, an addition to Young's Bristol property, happily remains as one of the city's showpieces.

CHILDREN REMEMBERED

On the borders of Oxfordshire and Warwickshire the road from Banbury to Stratford comes to the escarpment of Edgehill where Sir Edmund Verney bore the standard for Charles I at the battle in 1642, and a hundred years later Sanderson Miller erected his 'Gothick' tower on the hilltop. Less than a mile away stands Upton House, containing the famous Bearsted collection of paintings, and amongst the pictures there is a very small canvas by Hogarth showing a child in a cradle, with a doll and a little dog. There is nothing remarkable about the painting itself but on the back there is a piece of faded handwriting that connects this baby with a monument and a destroyed house forty miles away in Leicestershire, for it tells us that the baby's mother was Mary Edwards of Welham.

Anyone crossing the Welland bridge from Northampton-shire into Leicestershire, between Rockingham and Market Harborough, will notice that the village of Welham has a remarkable series of walls. These are not ordinary village walls but have an air of importance as if they belonged to a great house, and there are gate piers that lead to nothing but an empty pasture. When following a clue of this kind it is always wise to refer to local histories and have a look at the church, and in this case the evidence supplied by Nichols and Throsby, to-gether with the Edwards monument and the Hogarth painting, provide all that is needed to reconstruct the story of the walls of Welham.

The main feature of interest in Welham church is the Edwards monument, brought indoors from the churchyard in 1810 and now filling a north transept specially built for it. Throsby, writing at the end of the eighteenth century, when it was outside, described it as 'railed around with iron which has preserved it from the attack of boys'.[10] In its rather cramped position you can still see the marks of the iron railing, and the four great urns occupy the corners of the rather strange mausoleum, with the central obelisk rising to the roof. Around the base there are inscriptions to several generations of the Edwards family, including Gerard who died in 1743, forty years after Hogarth had painted him as a baby in his cradle. He was called 'Handsome Edwards' and married Lady Jane Noel, whose family we shall be considering when we go to Exton, and who survived him by thirty-eight years as Lord of the Manor of Welham.

Evidence of Lady Jane's long 'reign' at Welham is to be found on a memorial in the churchyard to 'Samuel Reeve, agent for thirty years to the Right Honourable Lady Jane Edwards', and on an old charity board inside the church, under the great weight that hangs from the clock in the belfry. These lists of bequests are always worth reading, and in view of the clock overhead, this one is most apt, for it refers to Lady Jane in connection with 'land in the lordship of Slawston, called Welham Church Clock Allotment, containing 1 acre and 20 poles'. Her own epitaph was added to the Edwards monument when she died in 1811, but the family mansion had already gone to decay, for Nichols writing earlier had already described the gardens as having been 'magnificent but now merely pasture within the walls'. He tells us that Francis Edwards, the grandfather of Hogarth's cradle child, had ambitious schemes for a turnpike road from Leicester to London, passing through Welham, and he built an inn for travellers, but the route of the new road was never approved and the inn was converted into the Edwards mansion.[11]

It is a pity that only broken walls remain from the great

house at Welham for it must have been an attractive place in its day. Francis Edwards went so far as to create a watercourse in front of the houses in the village and Nichols says that this gave the place quite a Dutch look, which is interesting because Edwards had married a Dutch wife. Perhaps for her sake he wanted to make these water-meadows by the Welland look like a little corner of Holland. In spite of the loss of the house those lengths of wall retain a certain dignity. In front of the cottages there is a long depression in the field, still called 'the canal', and the clock ticks loudly above the name of Lady Jane when you go into the church to find the memorial to her husband who, as a child, in spite of a doll and a dog to amuse him, looked very crossly at William Hogarth.

Mention of the Noel family recalls a story of people and events which is abundantly illustrated by monuments, and one which is also concerned with destroyed houses. Chipping Campden is one of the most-visited places in the Cotswolds, and the beauty of its long street reaches its climax at the approach to the church where the roadway is flanked on one side by a handsome row of almshouses on a raised causeway and on the other by the lodges and gateway of a great house. But the house has gone, and for the people who once lived here we must turn to the church and to the monument of Sir Baptist Hicks, Chipping Campden's great benefactor.

At the same time that the buildings of Wadham College were rising 'on the other side of Isis', Hicks was undertaking building projects at Campden, and it is to him that we owe that noble row of almshouses and, facing them, the few remaining fragments of Campden House. Behind the lodges and entrance arch there are other buildings and some ruins in an orchard, as well as two delightful pavilions which are best seen from the fields by the churchyard (p 124). It seems a far cry from this picture in golden Cotswold stone to the urban scenes of London W8, but the names of roads between Holland Park and Kensington Gardens will be a reminder that Hicks was at that time building another Campden House. He also gave the Jacobean pulpit in Campden church, inscribed 'Ex dono Benigni Baptistae Hickes', and the lovely fifteenth-century eagle lectern, and in his later years he built the Market House that makes such a valuable punctuation mark in the long and eloquent sentence of Campden's High Street. In that same street the heraldic sign of the Noel Arms is a reminder that it was this family that succeeded to the estate and title when Baptist Hicks, who had become Viscount Campden, died in 1629.

In the south-east chapel of Chipping Campden church there is an enormous monument to Baptist Hicks, a 'twelve-poster' arrangement in black and white marble, with Hicks and his wife recumbent in their state robes beneath a lofty canopy. The figures are superbly detailed, yet another instance of that wonderful period of Charles I, and are almost certainly by Nicholas Stone who did the monument at Watford to Hicks's daughter, Maria, and her husband Sir Charles Morrison. The other daughter and co-heiress was Juliana who married Sir Edward Noel, from a family with extensive estates in Leicestershire and Rutland, and it was he who was allowed to assume the title of 2nd Viscount Campden. The strange and rather macabre monument to Edward and Juliana stands at the south side of the chapel and has two life-size shrouded figures in white marble stepping out, hand in hand, from a dark recess with the doors flung open (p 127). It is signed by Joshua Marshall, though he spells his name 'Josuah', and the death of Sir Edward Noel is recorded as taking place at Oxford 'at the beginning of the late Fatall Civill Warrs, wither he went to serve and assist his Sovereign Prince, Charles the First'. These great inscribed doors of marble also tell us that the monument was erected in Juliana's lifetime, in 1664, so this is another example of commemoration of a loyal subject, after the Restoration, when it was safe to do so.

Juliana survived her husband for thirty-eight years and died in 1680 at Brooke, then in Rutland, one of the seats of the

Noel family, of which only an arch and a pretty octagonal gate-house remain. Brooke is a sweet place with honey-coloured cottages and a grey church in a green hollow not far from Oakham. The church is a lovely, unspoilt and important building for, in addition to some nice Norman features, it was largely rebuilt and refurnished in Elizabethan days, a rare thing amongst English churches. There is a handsome Jacobean monument to Charles Noel, brother-in-law to Juliana, who died young in 1619, more than sixty years before Juliana's body was taken from Brooke to Chipping Campden and those heavy marble doors were opened; for tradition has it that they were kept closed until she was laid to rest beside Sir Edward. However, it seems that the doors to this monument were still sometimes closed as late as 1696, for that was the year when Celia Fiennes visited 'Camden Town', as she calls it in her diary, 'to see the Effigie of the little Viscountess Camden that lived to a great age . . . its cut out in white marble . . . with two leav'd doores to it, to keep it from the dust'.[12] Juliana's steward at Campden, William Harrison, was the subject of the famous murder trial known as 'The Campden Wonder', in which, after a fantastic series of confessions and withdrawal of confessions, a couple named Perry were hanged at the gibbet on Broadway Hill for the murder of Harrison, although the body was never found. William Harrison turned up in Chipping Campden two years later with an even more fantastic story of how he had spent the intervening years.[13]

The Marshalls, father and son, were important sculptors and masons, each in his turn becoming Master Mason to the Crown under Charles II, although Joshua the son died only three years after his father Edward, whose work we noted at The Vyne and on the Verney tomb at Middle Claydon in Buckinghamshire. Also in that county is the Curwen monument at Amersham in which Edward Marshall used the resurrection theme of the shrouded figure emerging from open doors, long before his son developed this idea. This theme occurs again in several places including the Palmer memorial at East Carlton, Northants, which unfortunately is not signed. It is probable that one of the Marshalls did the East Carlton work, for not only is it very similar to the Campden one but also, according to Nichols, Sir Geoffrey Palmer's sister married Alexander Noel, brother to the 2nd Viscount Campden. Nichols adds a nice touch when he tells us that Sir Geoffrey Palmer was sent to the Tower on suspicion of plotting against Cromwell, and thereafter he could not bring himself to write 'Oliver' with a capital O!

Joshua Marshall is of special interest because he was involved in the rebuilding of London after the Great Fire, being master mason for the Monument on Fish Street Hill, also for the rebuilding of several city churches. He made the memorial in Westminster Abbey to the little princes who were killed in the Tower in 1483, and the pedestal for Le Sueur's statue of Charles I at the top of Whitehall.[14] Edward Marshall, the father, had worked under Nicholas Stone, so perhaps it was from him that the idea of the standing shrouded figure came, for Stone had done the famous figure of John Donne, happily saved from the ashes of Old St Paul's, for which the poet had posed in his shroud. The Marshalls' own memorial tablet is in London, at St Dunstan's in the West, for their sculptors' yard was at the corner of Fleet Street and Fetter Lane.

The burning of Campden House during the Civil War is not recorded on Marshall's monument to Juliana and her husband but on that of their son, Baptist Noel, 3rd Viscount Campden, at Exton, Leicestershire, formerly in Rutland, a great work by Gibbons which we have already referred to briefly because of its connections with Belvoir Castle and the Manners tombs at Bottesford. As so often happened after the disastrous effects of the Civil War, there was a move from one estate to another, and the family seat was established many miles away. Chipping Campden is seventy miles from Exton, but for the Noels this was in the nature of a home-coming for it was in Rutland and the adjoining counties that most of their property lay. Their memorials occur at Brooke and Whitwell, as well as at Old Dalby, Kirkby Mallory and Scraptoft in Leicestershire, and many other places, but it was Exton that became the chief seat of that branch of the family from which came the earls of Gainsborough. It is at Exton that the art of the sculptor demonstrates the way in which Noels followed Haringtons, after the marriage of Andrew Noel, of Dalby and Brooke, to Mabel Harington of Exton, and the distinguished series of monuments traces the changes in taste and fashion from the close of the medieval tradition to the late eighteenth century, and on to twentieth-century tablets.

Exton is a suitable place at which to end these journeys because it has all the ingredients that we have come to associate with monuments and their story, and the village is one of the most attractive in this part of the limestone belt that extends from the Cotswolds into the east Midlands. Its thatched stone-built cottages stand round a green that lies in the shade of a noble group of trees, but the church takes no part in this scene, being some distance away in the park, like so many others that we have visited in search of monuments. It would be hard to find were it not for a helpful sign, like that at Gayhurst, and when at last you come to it you are surprised to find such a large building with a soaring spire, so different from the usual 'park church' that hides discreetly amongst the outbuildings of the big house. At first the house is nowhere to be seen, but in fact there are two, the old mansion of the Haringtons and Noels, now a romantic ruin near the church, and the later Exton Park, largely of the nineteenth century, much farther away. To get the full effect of this great estate you should approach it from Oakham along the magnificent Barnsdale Avenue which ends up at the entrance to Exton Park, with heraldic gates bearing coloured and gilded shields with the familiar Noel arms (or, fretty gules, a canton ermine) that we saw on that inn sign in Chipping Campden.

It is tempting to deal with all the Exton monuments in detail, for this church is a treasure-house of English sculpture and there is much to be seen in addition to the outstanding memorial to Baptist Noel, the son of Sir Edward the Royalist and Juliana the Hicks heiress shown in their shrouds at Campden. There is a pre-Reformation altar tomb from the prolific 'school' of the Trent Valley alabastermen, a delightful thing, full of fun as well as fine carving; a later Harington tomb that tells of links by marriage with the Sidneys of Penshurst and the Montagus of Boughton as well as the all-important Noel link; another showing the Harington connection with Judge Kelway, which is one of the most technically accomplished of all Elizabethan works; a noble black-and-white marble tomb in the Nicholas Stone or Marshall tradition, and Noel monuments that take the story up to the classical work of Nollekens, with some excellent portrait medallions. But what we have really come to see at Exton is the great Gibbons work which fills one side of the north transept (p 107).

Few monuments are as informative as that of the 3rd Viscount Campden. It gives an exact account of his four marriages and his nineteen children as well as the reference to his losses in the Civil War so vividly linking Exton with Chipping Campden.

His eminent Loyalty to his Sovereigns King Charles I and II, his Conjugal Affection to Four Wives, his Paternal Indulgence to Nineteen Children: his Hospitality and Liberality to all that desired or deserved it, notwithstanding inestimable losses in his Estate, frequent Imprisonments of his Person, Spoil and Havoc of several of his Houses, besides the Burning of the Noble Pile of Campden . . .

What is so exceptional on Baptist Noel's monument is the portrayal of all these children, whether living at the time it was erected in 1686 or deceased, and whether they died in infancy or were stillborn, and a record of their marriages, including the reference to 'Catherine now wife of John Earl of Rutland' which we noted earlier as making a link with the portraits at

Belvoir and the similar Gibbons monument at Bottesford. It would be a long but rewarding exercise to trace all the family connections mentioned on this Exton monument, and to do it by means of portraits and monuments all over the country. To take only a few, we could start with Baptist Noel's first wife, Ann Fielding, who has her own memorial at Campden and earlier family ones at Monks Kirby in Warwickshire. His second wife, also Ann, was the widow of a Bourchier, Earl of Bath, recalling the series of monuments at Tawstock in North Devon; and the fourth wife 'who standeth by his side' was a Bertie from Grimsthorpe whose father's memorial we noted amongst all the others at Edenham. One of Noel's sons married a Wriothesley, which recalls our earlier journey to Titchfield and the portraits at Belvoir, emphasising the closely knit pattern of connections by marriage amongst the English aristocracy.

There is also a case of duplication in the north transept at Exton, for one of the children, shown on the exquisite little panels that Gibbons placed below the main figures, has his own monument on the opposite wall. He wears the strange hybrid garb that combines classical draperies and Roman footwear with the fashionable wig, cravat and long coat. In the midst of a Latin inscription there is an informative English verse that tells us that he died, in 1681, before reaching manhood, and offers a sidelong comment on the life and times of the reign of Charles II.

> Sprightly his meen, yet grave, discreet and wise
> Free from the age's Grand Debaucherys
> Vertue with Stature still his years out ran
> He dyd in's nonage and yet lived a man.

We have devoted some time to the monuments at Exton because of all our churches there are, as Pevsner has said, 'few in England where English sculpture from the 16th century to the 18th century can be studied so profitably and enjoyed so much',[15] and because a series of this richness seems to sum up so many of the points that have concerned us on these journeys. Here is costume, from the 'kennel' headdress of the time of Henry VII to the elaborate coiffure that one associates with Reynolds and Gainsborough, here is the story of the Civil War, the destroyed house, the link with portraits and monuments elsewhere, landscaping in the Cotswolds and in Rutland, and the colourful clues provided by heraldry on tombs, park gates and inn signs, as well as the banners and tabards of arms that hang high up in the lofty clerestory of the church in the park. To stand by the gate into the grounds and contemplate the sun-warmed and rain-washed fragments of the old Exton manor house, just as we did at Chipping Campden and Moreton Corbet, and then go and look at the people themselves in their ruffs and caps, their wigs and bonnets, is to feel acutely a sense of history. One could criticise the scale and the extravagance of a monument like that of Baptist Noel, 3rd Viscount Campden, with its gigantic urns and Roman figures, but what could be lovelier than those subsidiary panels (p 127) with that gay white company of children, the older ones leading the toddlers in a perpetual country dance, as crisp and delicate as when they were carved in the days of Gibbons and Wren, Newton and Kneller, and in the England of Dryden and Locke, Purcell and Pepys?

NOTES AND REFERENCES

Chapter 1

1 Byng, John. *The Torrington Diaries.* ed C. Bruyn Andrews. London: Eyre & Spottiswoode, 1954
2 Whistler, Laurence. *Vanbrugh: Architect and Dramatist.* London: Cobden-Sanderson, 1938
3 Pevsner mentions another instance of strange spelling, on the Scheemakers monument to Sir Samuel Ongley at Old Warden, Beds. 'P. Chiemaker en L. Delvaux Inventor et Fecit'. He adds the comment, 'It must be Delvaux's spelling, and whose is the Latin?' (*The Buildings of England: Bedfordshire, Huntingdon and Peterborough*)
4 Graham, Rigby and Holt, Penelope. 'A Sentimental Journey', *The American Book Collector,* Vol 21 No 5. Chicago, 1971
5 Byng, op cit
6 Barbeau, A. *Life and Letters at Bath in the 18th Century.* London: Heinemann, 1904
7 Pembroke, 16th Earl of. *Guide to Wilton House.* London: Pitkin, 1970
8 Ibid
9 *Dictionary of National Biography.* 'Sable hearse' in some other versions
10 Gunnis, Rupert. *Dictionary of British Sculptors: 1660–1851.* London: Odhams, 1953
11 *DNB*
12 Sackville-West, V. *Knole and the Sackvilles.* London: Benn, 1958
13 Ibid

Chapter 2

1   *DNB*
2   Burton, Elizabeth. *The Georgians at Home*. London: Longmans, 1967
3   Bolton, Arthur T. Article on Croome in *Country Life*, 10 April 1915
4   Several Coventry portraits are to be seen at Antony House, Cornwall, for the builder of the house, Sir William Carew, married Lady Anne, the heiress of Gilbert, 4th Earl of Coventry of Croome Court. In the entrance hall at Antony there is a portrait by Cornelius Johnson of Lord Keeper Coventry, the subject of the earliest of the Croome monuments, and there are others by Dahl of the builder of the house and his Coventry wife. Others are on the staircase, and there are sporting paintings from Croome in the dining-room.
5   Green, David. *Grinling Gibbons*. London: Country Life, 1964
6   The actual words describing this incident appear on an additional inscription at the side of the monument:

> This Tomb was carried to ye Church of Croome Dabitot there to be Erected but the Earl of Coventry Son to ye Right Honorable ye deceased denying it to be set up ye Countess Dowager at whose charge it was made being the wife to Thomas Savage of Elmley Castle Esq it was by his order brought to this place.

7   The spelling of the surname, with or without the 'e', seems to have been of no consequence, for it appears in both forms on these Warwick tablets.
8   Gunnis, Rupert. *Dictionary of British Sculptors*. London: Odhams, 1953
9   Girouard, Mark. *Robert Smythson and the Architecture of the Elizabethan Era*. London: Country Life, 1966
10 Williams, Ethel Carleton. *Bess of Hardwick*. London: Longmans, 1959
11 Girouard, op cit
12 Ibid
13 Throsby, John. *Select Views in Leicestershire*. 1789
14 Byng, op cit
15 Moir, Esther. *The Discovery of Britain*. London: Routledge, 1964

16 Stroud, Dorothy. *Capability Brown*. London: Country Life, 1957

Chapter 3
1 Walpole, Horace. *Selected Letters*. ed William Hadley. London: Dent (Everyman), 1963
2 Gunnis, op cit
3 *DNB*
4 Rowse, A. L. *Shakespeare's Southampton*. London: Macmillan, 1965
5 Dare, M. P. *Guide to Bottesford Church*. Gloucester: British Publishing Co, 1949
6 Ibid

Chapter 4
1 Walpole, op cit
2 Pevsner, N. *The Buildings of England: Buckinghamshire*. Harmondsworth: Penguin, 1960
3 *DNB*
4 Introduction to Esdaile, K. A. *English Church Monuments: 1510 to 1840*. London: Batsford, 1946
5 Byng, op cit
6 Lines, Charles. *Stanford Hall: A Family Portrait*. Leamington: English Counties Periodicals
7 Nichols, John. *History and Antiquities of Leicestershire*. 1795–1811
8 Strong, Roy. *The Elizabethan Image*. Catalogue of Exhibition at Tate Gallery, London, 1969
9 Jenkins, Elizabeth. *Elizabeth and Leicester*. London: Gollancz, 1961

Chapter 5
1 Collinson, Rev John. *The History of Somersetshire*. 1791
2 *The Journeys of Celia Fiennes*. ed Christopher Morris. London: Cresset Press, 1949
3 *The Verneys of Claydon*. ed Sir Harry Verney. Oxford: Maxwell, 1968
4 *The Journeys of Celia Fiennes*
5 Lipscombe, G. *The History and Antiquities of the County of Buckingham*. London: Robins, 1847

6 *The Verneys of Claydon*

7 Connor, Arthur B. *Monumental Brasses in Somerset*. Bath: Kingsmead Reprints, 1970

8 Fuller, Thomas. *The History of the Worthies of England*. 1662

9 Connor, op cit

10 Throsby, John. *Supplementary Volume to the Leicestershire Views*. 1790

11 Nichols, John. *History and Antiquities of Leicestershire*. 1795–1811

12 *The Journeys of Celia Fiennes*

13 *The Campden Wonder*. ed Sir George Clark. London: Oxford University Press, 1959

14 Gunnis, op cit

15 Pevsner, N. *The Buildings of England: Leicestershire and Rutland*. Harmondsworth: Penguin, 1960

APPENDIX 1

POST-REFORMATION MONUMENTS —STYLES AND PERIODS

Monuments tell the story of English taste and fashion over a long period; even if the sequence is confined to post-Reformation examples, they provide a continuous record of the changes in costume and artistic style during three hundred years. For the sake of brevity the story can be reduced to five main periods, and the recognition of these will help in the understanding of a wonderful pageant of history.

ELIZABETHAN AND JACOBEAN

Second half of the sixteenth century and early seventeenth century

In the middle of the sixteenth century the introduction of Renaissance ideas gradually superseded Gothic forms, and the traditions of medieval art began to disappear, a process accelerated by the destruction of the monasteries and the other changes in the Church, in politics and economics. The break with Rome resulted in the new Renaissance elements in design coming from northern Europe rather than direct from Italy, so architectural forms in buildings, furniture and monuments were of a robust character, lacking the purity of truly classical motifs. In monuments the recumbent pose, with hands held in an attitude of prayer, gives an almost medieval feeling to these Elizabethan and Jacobean figures, but the abundance of columns, obelisks, strap-work and grotesques (pp 72, 108), sometimes making a great four-poster, six-poster or even an eight-poster pavilion (p 90), was a break-away from the Gothic forms still being used in the Early Tudor works of the reigns of Henry VII and Henry VIII. Lettering was usually in the Roman style, appropriate to Renaissance ideas, but the old Gothic 'black letter' continued for a long time in provincial work.

Alabaster was the commonest material, often painted and gilded, and when combined with a lofty heraldic superstructure the effect was very rich. As well as the traditional recumbent pose there was a tendency to show figures as in life, kneeling on either side of a prayer desk, particularly in the smaller mural monuments which became common. In all types the children were shown kneeling at the base, or at each end. Another attempt to show figures as in life resulted in a curious, stiffly reclining position, leaning on one elbow with a hand supporting the head.

Men are shown with short hair and beard, with a deep, outstanding ruff at the neck (p 72), and armour is often worn, or else a' richly ornamental doublet and trunk hose, padded and slashed. Women show the hair-styles associated with Elizabethan portraits, with a close-fitting cap or sometimes a hood of immense size, and occasionally a broad-brimmed hat. A high, upstanding collar is sometimes found as an alternative to the ruff, and dresses often have slashed sleeves, and skirts falling stiffly from a wide farthingale (p 131).

The most notable sculptors were those of the Southwark group, originating from the Netherlands: the Johnsons or Janssens, Colt and the Cures.

CAROLEAN AND COMMONWEALTH

Mid-seventeenth century

Many of the Elizabethan and Jacobean features continue, indeed there are monuments with some very bizarre elements, but classical motifs become a little more refined while obelisks, strapwork and the rather gross ornament of the previous period gradually disappeared. Recumbent, kneeling and stiffly reclining figures (p 109) continued but a new design appeared, with a bust or head and shoulders framed in an oval opening. Sometimes the opening, with an architectural surround, was developed into a sort of tent or pavilion with curtains held back. The ruff gave place to the falling collar (p 36) and the most intricate lace and ribbons appeared on the dress of men and women. Armour still occurs and men have the hair longer, with the pointed beard associated with portraits of Charles I, while women are shown with ringlets as in Van Dyck and Lely paintings.

The decade of the 1630s produced some of the most accomplished monuments in the history of English sculpture (p 128), and white and black marble began to compete with alabaster as the material favoured by sculptors. This is the period of Nicholas Stone and his followers, of Edward and Joshua Marshall and the Christmas family.

LATE STUART AND EARLY GEORGIAN

From the Restoration to William and Mary, Anne and George I

At the Restoration of the monarchy in 1660 a new era began for the arts in England; the return of the court brought continental influences and Charles II was anxious to emulate his father's patronage of the arts. A more scholarly attitude to classical design is to be seen in architecture, furniture and monuments, but there is still a vigorous element of experiment which, in monuments, resulted in a baroque treatment of architectural surrounds with curved or broken pediments, cherubs and heraldry. Marble superseded alabaster, and armour no longer appeared except in a few rare instances.

This is the period of the life-size figures of noblemen, lawyers and country squires, standing or carelessly reclining, in contemporary costume, the men having the long curly periwig, long buttoned coat and square-toed shoes (p 89). Women are often shown with a daring decolletage above ample draperies with billowing folds. Architectural backgrounds reached their most splendid development (p 89) and the largest monuments usually have allegorical figures such as Justice, Truth, Faith or Hope, flanking the main subject (p 36).

Although contemporary costume was the general rule up to the beginning of the reign of George II, with some of the more advanced sculptors there was a tendency even as early as the 1680s to represent their patrons in the heroic Roman manner (p 107), but this properly belongs to the next period. Public statues of Charles II often show him dressed as a Roman emperor yet wearing a full-bottomed wig, and this curious mixture occurs on monuments by such men as Grinling Gibbons, his collaborator Quellin, and John Nost. Other sculptors of the period include Thomas Green of Camberwell, Cibber, Francis Bird. Bushnell and the Stanton family.

THE ROMAN MANNER

Mid-eighteenth century

The enthusiasm for Antiquity and the doctrine of the Ideal and Heroic led to figures on monuments being dressed as Romans, sometimes in armour or else loosely wrapped in a toga-like garment. They are found standing, or reclining on a sarcophagus (p 54), in association with urns, portrait busts, putti (little boys, like wingless cherubs) and medallions, usually with a black marble pyramid shape for a background. This preoccupation with the cold, correct classical style was parallel to the Palladian movement in architecture and led to the abandonment of the more emotional Baroque, depriving us of contemporary costume in monuments, except in a few rare cases.

The Grand Tour made the English aristocracy familiar with classical culture and many returned with antique busts and figures, and with paintings and engravings of classical scenes. This emphasis on all that was Roman led the gentry and the country squires to emulate the buildings of antiquity in their houses and parks, while on their monuments they appear as a reincarnation of the emperors (p 17). Fortunately they did allow a measure of reality in the small portrait medallions that frequently accompany these imposing groups, so we are able to catch a glimpse of the short wigs for men and the high hair-styles of the women, reminiscent of the portraits by Reynolds, Gainsborough, Zoffany, Ramsay, Romney and the rest.

Another influx of foreign sculptors had a great influence on monuments, though some of them worked in collaboration with English architects such as Gibbs and Kent. The important sculptors of this period include Roubiliac, Rysbrack, the Scheemakers family, Cheere and Wilton.

LATE GEORGIAN AND REGENCY

Late eighteenth century and early nineteenth century

Towards the end of the eighteenth century, from about 1770, the new discoveries of archaeologists at Pompeii and Herculaneum, and particularly in Greece, led monumental sculptors to follow a more restrained style, and the purity of Greek art came to be much admired. With some sculptors this Neo-Classicism produced a sameness in design, and the mourning female figure bent over an urn became repetitive (p 35). However, there were other themes which showed vitality and variety, and the number of important sculptors increased, including Nollekens, the Bacons, Flaxman, Banks, the Westmacotts and Chantrey.

As in architecture, the enthusiasm for everything Greek was not without competition. The spirit of archaeology encouraged a new interest in our own past so that Gothic became fashionable too, as a sort of romantic alternative to the scholarly world of classical art. Except for naval and military figures, of which there are many, we find that costume on monuments is restricted to a non-committal arrangement of draperies with a timeless classicism, but contemporary dress does occasionally appear.

In general, classical design held the field during Georgian and Regency times, but the Victorian era saw the supremacy of the revived Gothic (p 128), and the story of English monumental art came to an end with reproductions of earlier designs of which the most ambitious endeavoured to recreate the spirit of the Middle Ages.

APPENDIX 2

COUNTY LISTS OF MONUMENTS

A selected list of churches that contain monuments of interest, either as groups of family memorials or important individual works. Some major medieval monuments and brasses have been included. The counties shown are those established under the new arrangements in operation from 1 April 1974. To facilitate reference to books and maps published under the earlier system, where changes have occurred the old county is shown in parentheses.

AVON

Almondsbury (Glos)
Badminton (Glos)
Bath Abbey (Som)
Bristol Cathedral
——, Lord Mayor's Chapel
——, St Mary Redcliffe
——, St Stephen
Camerton (Som)
Chew Magna (Som)
Churchill (Som)

Clapton-in-Gordano (Som)
Dyrham (Glos)
Harptree, East (Som)
Keynsham (Som)
Long Ashton (Som)
Tortworth (Glos)
Wellow (Som)
Winterbourne (Glos)
Yatton (Som)

BEDFORDSHIRE

Bletsoe
Blunham
Bromham
Campton
Cardington
Colmworth

Dunstable
Eyeworth
Flitton
Holcot
Luton
Marston Moretaine

BEDFORDSHIRE

Maulden
Old Warden
Sutton
Toddington

Turvey
Willington
Wymington

BERKSHIRE

Aldermaston
Aldworth
Arborfield
Bisham
Englefield
Eton College Chapel (Bucks)
Hurst
Lambourn
Langley Marish (Bucks)

Pangbourne
Reading, St Laurence
Sonning
Speen
Tilehurst
Windsor, St John Baptist
Windsor Castle, St George's
    Chapel

BUCKINGHAMSHIRE

Amersham
Aylesbury
Beachampton
Castlethorpe
Chenies
Chicheley
Chilton
Clifton Reynes
Drayton Beauchamp

Fawley
Fulmer
Gayhurst
Grendon
    Underwood
Hambledon
High Wycombe
Hillesden
Hitcham

Iver
Lillingstone Dayrell
Long Crendon
Middle Claydon
Old Wolverton
Quainton
Ravenstone
Soulbury
Wing

CAMBRIDGESHIRE

Abington, Great
Babraham
Balsham
Bottisham
Cambridge, Caius College
    Chapel
——, Christ's College Chapel
——, Trinity College Chapel

Chesterton (Hunts)
Cheveley
Conington, St Mary
Conington, All Saints (Hunts)
Dullingham
Ely Cathedral
Harlton
Haslingfield

CAMBRIDGESHIRE

Horseheath
Isleham
Kirtling
Landwade
Linton
Long Stanton, All Saints
Longstowe
Madingley
Marholm (Peterborough)
Peterborough Cathedral
St Neots (Hunts)

Sawtry (Hunts)
Staughton, Great (Hunts)
Stetchworth
Swavesey
Thornhaugh (Peterborough)
Trumpington
Ufford (Peterborough)
Upton (Peterborough)
Westley Waterless
Wimpole
Wisbech

CHESHIRE

Acton
Barthomley
Bunbury
Chester, Cathedral
——, St Mary on
the Hill

Farnworth (Lancs)
Gawsworth
Macclesfield
Malpas
Over Peover

Rostherne
Tarporley
Warrington (Lancs)
Winwick (Lancs)

CLEVELAND

Guisborough (N Yorks)
Kirkleatham (N Yorks)
Norton-on-Tees (Durham)

CORNWALL

Lanreath
Launceston
Mevagissey
North Hill

Padstow
Pelynt
St Ewe
St Martin by Looe

St Mellion
St Michael Penkevil
St Tudy
Truro Cathedral

CUMBRIA

Appleby (Westmorland)
Carlisle Cathedral (Cumber-
land)
Cartmel (Lancs)

Kendal (Westmorland)
Lowther (Westmorland)
Ulverston (Lancs)
Wetheral (Cumberland)

DERBYSHIRE

Ashbourne
Bakewell
Bolsover
Chesterfield
Derby Cathedral
Duffield
Edensor

Elvaston
Hathersage
Kedleston
Longford
Morley
Newton Solney
Norbury

Radbourne
Sudbury
Tideswell
Wilne
Youlgreave

DEVON

Barnstaple
Berry Pomeroy
Broadclyst
Buckland
  Monachorum
Cadeleigh
Clovelly
Colyton

Crediton
Eggesford
Exeter Cathedral
Gittisham
Haccombe
Holcombe Rogus
Landkey
Newton St Cyres

Ottery St Mary
Paignton
Plympton
Tavistock
Tawstock
Wembury
Widworthy
Wolborough

DORSET

Beaminster
Chelborough, West
Christchurch Priory (Hants)
Cranborne
Dorchester St Peter
Frampton
Gillingham
Iwerne Courtney
Longburton
Mapperton

Melbury Sampford
Milton Abbas
Minterne Magna
Puddletown
Sherborne Abbey
Silton
Whitchurch Canonicorum
Wimborne Minster
Wimborne St Giles

DURHAM

Brancepeth
Chester-le-Street

Durham Cathedral
Staindrop

ESSEX

Arkesden
Baddow, Little
Boreham
Borley
Brightlingsea
Castle Hedingham
Chrishall
Colchester, St James the
   Greater
——, St Mary at the Walls
Dunmow, Little
Easton, Little
Faulkbourne
Felsted
Gosfield
Halstead

Hempstead
Ingatestone
Layer Marney
Maplestead, Great
Orsett
Rettendon
St Osyth
Stansted Mountfitchet
Steeple Bumpstead
Theydon Mount
Waltham Abbey
Waltham, Great
Warley, Little
Willingale Doe
Wivenhoe
Writtle

GLOUCESTERSHIRE

Ampney Crucis
Berkeley
Bishops Cleeve
Blockley
Chipping Campden
Cirencester
Coberley
Deerhurst
Ebrington

Fairford
Gloucester,
   Cathedral
——, St Nicholas
Hardwicke
Longborough
Minchinhampton
Miserden

Newland
Northleach
Sapperton
Sherborne
Shipton Moyne
Somerford Keynes
Tewkesbury Abbey
Wotton-under-Edge

HAMPSHIRE

Basing
Bramley
Catherington
Chawton
Farley
   Chamberlayne
Greatham

Hale
Highclere
Hurstbourne Priors
Ibsley
Kingsclere
Laverstoke
Northington

Nursling
Old Alresford
Portsmouth
   Cathedral
Romsey Abbey
Soberton
Stoneham, North

HAMPSHIRE

Stratfield Saye	Vyne, Chapel of the	Winchester
Thruxton	Warnford	Cathedral
Tichborne	Wickham	Woodhay, East
Titchfield	Wield	Wootton

HEREFORD AND WORCESTER

Astley (Worcs)	Holme Lacy (Hereford)
Bacton (Hereford)	Hope under Dinmore (Hereford)
Beoley (Worcs)	Kidderminster (Worcs)
Besford (Worcs)	Kinnersley (Hereford)
Birtsmorton (Worcs)	Ledbury (Hereford)
Bockleton (Worcs)	Leigh (Worcs)
Bosbury (Hereford)	Malvern Priory (Worcs)
Bredon (Worcs)	Much Marcle (Hereford)
Bromsgrove (Worcs)	Norton (Worcs)
Clehonger (Hereford)	Powick (Worcs)
Croft (Hereford)	Ross-on-Wye (Hereford)
Croome d'Abitot (Worcs)	Rous Lench (Worcs)
Eastnor (Hereford)	Spetchley (Worcs)
Eckington (Worcs)	Strensham (Worcs)
Elmley Castle (Worcs)	Tardebigge (Worcs)
Eye (Hereford)	Tyberton (Hereford)
Fladbury (Worcs)	Weobley (Hereford)
Hampton Lovett (Worcs)	Wichamford (Worcs)
Hanbury (Worcs)	Witley, Great (Worcs)
Hereford Cathedral	Worcester Cathedral

HERTFORDSHIRE

Abbots Langley	Hertingfordbury	St Albans, Cathedral
Aldenham	Hunsdon	——, St Michael
Bayford	Knebworth	Sawbridgeworth
Braughing	Mimms, South	Standon
Broxbourne	(Middx)	Tring
Gaddesden, Little	Offley	Watford
Hatfield		Wheathampstead

HUMBERSIDE

Adlingfleet (Yorks, West Riding)
Ashby cum Fenby (Lincs)
Beverley Minster (Yorks, East Riding)
Broughton (Lincs)
Burton Agnes (Yorks, East Riding)
Dalton, South (Yorks, East Riding)
Ferriby, North (Yorks, East Riding)
Harpham (Yorks, East Riding)
Hull, Holy Trinity (Yorks, East Riding)
Kirk Ella (Yorks, East Riding)
Lockington (Yorks, East Riding)
Lowthorpe (Yorks, East Riding)
Stallingborough (Lincs)
Swine (Yorks, East Riding)
Warter (Yorks, East Riding)

ISLE OF WIGHT

Arreton
Brading
Godshill
Newport
Shorwell
Yarmouth

KENT

Ash, St Nicholas
Ashford
Aylesford
Betteshanger
Birchington
Boughton Monchelsea
Boughton-under-Blean
Brasted
Brenchley
Canterbury, Cathedral
——, St Margaret
Chartham
Chevening
Chilham
Cobham
Dartford
Eastchurch
Eastwell (removed to Victoria & Albert Museum)
Faversham, St Catherine
——, St Mary
Goudhurst
Hever
Hinxhill
Hollingbourne
Hothfield
Hunton
Ightham
Linton
Lullingstone
Lynsted
Maidstone, All Saints
Malling, West
Mereworth

KENT

Minster-in-Sheppey
Northbourne
Otford
Otterden
Penshurst
Rainham
Rochester Cathedral
Shipbourne
Southfleet
Sutton-at-Hone
Sutton, East
Swanscombe
Tunstall
Waldershare
Wateringbury
Wingham
Yalding

LANCASHIRE

Mitton (Yorks, West Riding)   Ormskirk

LEICESTERSHIRE

Ashby-de-la-Zouch
Ashby Folville
Bottesford
Breedon-on-the-Hill
Brooke (Rutland)
Brooksby
Castle Donington
Edmondthorpe
Exton (Rutland)
Fenny Drayton
Frolesworth
Kirkby Mallory
Leicester Cathedral
Lockington
Noseley
Prestwold
Quorn
Shepshed
Stapleford
Stoke Dry (Rutland)
Theddingworth
Thurlaston
Wistow

LINCOLNSHIRE

Alford
Belton
Bigby
Boston
Brocklesby
Carlton, South
Cockerington, South
Denton
Edenham
Gautby
Glentworth
Grantham
Hainton
Heydour
Irnham
Kelstern
Laughton
Lincoln Cathedral
Linwood
Marston
Nocton
Norton Disney
Rand
Rippingale

LINCOLNSHIRE

Sleaford
Snarford
Spilsby
Stamford, All Saints

——, St Martin
——, St Mary
Stoke, South
Tathwell

Tattershall
Uffington
Whaplode
Wrangle

LONDON, Greater

Addington (Surrey)
Barking (Essex)
Barnet (Herts)
Battersea, St Mary
Beddington (Surrey)
Carshalton (Surrey)
Cheam (Surrey)
Chelsea, All Saints
Chiswick (Middx)
Clapham, St Paul
Cranford (Middx)
Crayford (Kent)
Croydon (Surrey)
Enfield (Middx)
Erith (Kent)
Finsbury, St John Clerkenwell
——, Charterhouse Chapel
Fulham, All Saints
Greenwich, St Luke Charlton
Hackney, St John
Hammersmith, St Paul
Hampton (Middx)

Harefield (Middx)
Hayes (Middx)
Hillingdon (Middx)
Lewisham, St Mary
Leyton (Essex)
Ockendon, North (Essex)
Romford (Essex)
St Bartholomew, Smithfield
St Helen, Bishopsgate
St Paul's Cathedral
Southwark Cathedral
Stanmore, Great (Middx)
Stanmore, Little (Whitchurch)
  (Middx)
Tottenham (Middx)
Uxbridge (Middx)
Walthamstow (Essex)
Wanstead (Essex)
West Ham (Essex)
Westminster, Abbey
——, St Margaret

MANCHESTER, Greater

Bowdon (Cheshire)
Cheadle (Cheshire)
Didsbury, St James

Manchester Cathedral
Standish (Lancs)
Stockport, St Mary (Cheshire)

K

MERSEYSIDE
Prescot (Lancs)
Sefton (Lancs)

MIDLANDS, West
Aston (Warks)
Halesowen (Worcs)
Handsworth (Warks)

Sutton Coldfield (Warks)
Wolverhampton (Staffs)

NORFOLK
Acre, South
Ashwellthorpe
Barningham, North
Besthorpe
Blickling
Dereham, West
Elsing
Emneth
Felbrigg
Harling, East
Hethel
Hingham
Holkham
Hunstanton
Ingham
Ketteringham
King's Lynn, St Margaret
Langford
Loddon

Marham
Narborough
Norwich, Cathedral
——, St Andrew
——, St George Colegate
——, St Peter, Permountergate
Oxborough
Oxnead
Paston
Reepham
Snettisham
Spixworth
Sprowston
Stow Bardolph
Tittleshall
Walsham, North
Walsingham, Little
Wickhampton
Woodrising

NORTHAMPTONSHIRE
Apethorpe
Ashby St Ledgers
Barnwell, All Saints
Billing, Great
Braybrooke
Brington, Great

Carlton, East
Castle Ashby
Charwelton
Clipston
Cottesbrooke
Courteenhall

Deene
Dodford
Easton Maudit
Easton Neston
Edgcote
Fawsley

NORTHAMPTONSHIRE

Greens Norton
Hardingstone
Harrington
Higham Ferrers
Horton
Lowick
Maidwell
Norton
Paulerspury

Rockingham
Rushton
Southwick
Spratton
Stanford-on-Avon
Steane
Stoke Doyle
Stow Nine
   Churches

Thorpe Achurch
Thorpe Mandeville
Titchmarsh
Warkton
Warkworth
Weekley
Whiston

NORTHUMBERLAND

Chillingham
Warkworth

NOTTINGHAMSHIRE

Averham
Barton-in-Fabis
Blyth
Bunny
Clifton
Holme
Holme Pierrepont
Kelham
Kingston-on-Soar
Langar
Newark
Newstead Abbey
Ossington

Ratcliffe-on-Soar
Screveton
Sibthorpe
Southwell Minster
Stapleford
Strelley
Teversal
Tuxford
Walkeringham
Willoughby-on-the-Wolds
Wollaton
Wysall

OXFORDSHIRE

Abingdon (Berks)
Bicester
Blenheim Chapel
Brightwell Baldwin
Broughton
Burford

Cogges
Coleshill (Berks)
Dorchester Abbey
Ewelme
Faringdon (Berks)
Lewknor

OXFORDSHIRE

Milton, Great
Oxford, Cathedral
——, Merton College Chapel
——, New College Chapel
——, Wadham College Chapel
Radley (Berks)
Rotherfield Greys
Shellingford (Berks)
Somerton
Sparsholt (Berks)
Spelsbury
Stanton Harcourt
Steeple Aston
Stratton Audley
Swinbrook
Tackley
Thame
Uffington (Berks)
Wheatfield
Wittenham, Little (Berks)
Wroxton
Yarnton

SHROPSHIRE

Acton Burnell
Acton Round
Albrighton, St Mary
    Magdalene
Aston Botterell
Badger
Burford
Cardington
Claverley
Condover
Hodnet
Kinlet
Ludford
Ludlow
Moreton Corbet
Moreton Say
Neen Sollars
Norton-in-Hales
Oswestry
Quatt
Shifnal
Shrewsbury, St Mary
——, Holy Cross
Stoke-upon-Tern
Tong
Worfield
Wroxeter

SOMERSET

Axbridge
Bishops Hull
Brent Knoll
Bridgwater
Bruton
Brympton d'Evercy
Cloford
Cothelstone
Curry Mallet
Curry Rivel
Dowlish Wake
Dunster
Farleigh Hungerford, Castle
    Chapel

SOMERSET

Frome
Goathurst
Hinton St George
Ilminster
Petherton, South
Pitminster
Porlock
Rodney Stoke

Stogumber
Stogursey
Taunton, St Mary Magdalene
Watchet
Wellington
Wells Cathedral
Wiveliscombe

STAFFORDSHIRE

Ashley
Blithfield
Blore
Brewood
Checkley
Church Leigh
Clifton Campville
Croxall

Eccleshall
Elford
Ilam
Ingestre
Lichfield Cathedral
Mavesyn Ridware
Norbury

Patshull
Penkridge
Sandon
Seighford
Stafford, St Mary
Tamworth
Yoxall

SUFFOLK

Acton
Ampton
Assington
Badingham
Barham
Boxted
Bramfield
Brent Eleigh
Brightwell
Brome
Bures, St Stephen's
  Chapel
Burgate
Bury St Edmunds,
  Cathedral
——, St Mary

Chilton
Cowlinge
Culford
Debenham
Denham, St Mary
Dennington
Elmswell
Framlingham
Hawstead
Helmingham
Hengrave
Holbrook
Hoxne
Ipswich, St Mary
  le Tower
——, St Stephen

Kedington
Long Melford
Milden
Mildenhall
Redgrave
Rendlesham
Rushbrooke
Saxham, Little
Sotterley
Stoke-by-Nayland
Stowlangtoft
Thurlow, Little
Westhorpe
Wickhambrook
Wingfield
Woodbridge

SURREY

Bletchingley
Bookham, Great
Egham
Ewell
Godstone
Guildford, Holy Trinity
———, St Nicholas
Horsell
Horsley, East
Horsley, West
Lingfield
Ockham
Peper Harow
Reigate
Stanwell (Middx)
Stoke d'Abernon
Walton-on-Thames
Wotton

SUSSEX, East

Ashburnham
Battle
Chiddingley
Etchingham
Firle, West
Fletching
Friston
Herstmonceux
Isfield
Pevensey
Warbleton
Willingdon
Winchelsea
Withyham

SUSSEX, West

Arundel
Boxgrove
Broadwater
Chichester
   Cathedral
Cowfold
Grinstead, West
Horsham
Racton
Slaugham (East
   Sussex)
Trotton
Wiston

TYNE AND WEAR

Newcastle Cathedral (Northumberland)
Sunderland, Holy Trinity (Durham)
Whitburn (Durham)

WARWICKSHIRE

Alcester
Astley
Baginton
Barcheston
Caldecote
Charlecote
Chesterton
Churchover
Coleshill
Compton Verney
Coughton
Ettington (old
   church)
Grendon
Honington

WARWICKSHIRE

Merevale
Middleton
Monks Kirby
Newbold-on-Avon
Nuneaton
Preston-on-Stour

Quinton
Shuckburgh, Upper
Stoneleigh
Stratford-on-Avon
Tanworth-in-Arden

Warwick, St Mary
Weston-on-Avon
Wixford
Wootton Wawen

WILTSHIRE

Aldbourne
Bedwyn, Great
Broad Hinton
Bromham
Charlton
Clyffe Pypard
Collingbourne
Kingston

Dauntsey
Downton
Draycot Cerne
Edington
Lacock
Lavington, West
Ludgershall

Lydiard Tregoze
Maiden Bradley
Ramsbury
Salisbury Cathedral
Stourton
Urchfont
West Dean

YORKSHIRE, North

Bedale
Coxwold
Croft
Gilling
Goldsborough (Yorks, West
Riding)
Hazlewood Castle Chapel
(Yorks, West Riding)
Healaugh (Yorks, West
Riding)
Hornby
Kirklington
Knaresborough (Yorks, West
Riding)
Ledsham (Yorks, West
Riding)

Masham
Richmond
Ripley (Yorks, West Riding)
Ripon Cathedral (Yorks, West
Riding)
Ryther (Yorks, West Riding)
Skipton (Yorks, West Riding)
Stanwick
Tanfield, West
Topcliffe
Wath
Well
Wighill (Yorks, West Riding)
York, Minster
——, St Michael le Belfrey

YORKSHIRE, South
  Darton (Yorks, West Riding)   Silkstone (Yorks, West Riding)
  Ecclesfield (Yorks, West   Tickhill (Yorks, West Riding)
    Riding)   Wentworth (Yorks, West
  Norton (Yorks, West Riding)   Riding)
  Sheffield Cathedral (Yorks,
    West Riding)

YORKSHIRE, West
  Harewood   Thornhill
  Kirkheaton   Wakefield Cathedral
  Methley   Whitkirk
  Otley

BIBLIOGRAPHY

Very little has been written on the subject of church monuments, and what has appeared is usually to be found in historical journals as monographs on individual sculptors or as material in the transactions of archaeological societies. In comparison with monumental brasses, made popular because of the practical appeal of making attractive rubbings, the list of books on monuments and sculptors, available for the general reader, is short indeed.

Esdaile, Katharine A. *English Church Monuments 1510–1840.* London: Batsford, 1946
——. *English Monumental Sculpture since the Renaissance.* London: SPCK, 1927
Gunnis, Rupert. *Dictionary of British Sculptors 1660–1851.* London: Odhams, 1953
Whinney, Margaret. *Sculpture in Britain 1530–1830.* (Pelican History of Art). Harmondsworth, Middx: Penguin, 1964
Green, David. *Grinling Gibbons.* London: Country Life, 1964

For aspects other than those which are the main concern of this study the reader is referred to the following.

Crossley, F. H. *English Church Monuments 1150–1550.* London: Batsford, 1921
Stone, L. *Sculpture in Britain; the Middle Ages* (Pelican History of Art). Harmondsworth: Penguin, 1955
Burgess, Frederick. *English Churchyard Memorials.* London: Lutterworth Press, 1963
Lindley, Kenneth. *Of Graves and Epitaphs.* London: Hutchinson, 1965

For the location of monuments, county by county, and brief notes on their place in English art history, the *Buildings of England* series, under the editorship of Sir Nikolaus Pevsner and published by Penguin, is indispensable. The *Shell Guides*, published by Faber, and some other county books deal briefly with monuments, and the many works on English costume will be helpful in a more detailed study of this aspect. Issues of *Country Life*, when dealing with historic houses, frequently make reference to family monuments, and for the background study of the people concerned the *Dictionary of National Biography* is a valuable source of information. Other books that touch upon some of the personalities involved are listed in the notes for each chapter.

INDEX

Places which occur only in the county lists in Appendix 2 are not included here.
Page references in italic refer to illustrations.

80
-1RO